Good Housekeeping's
PARTY PIE BOOK

by *the editors of* GOOD HOUSEKEEPING MAGAZINE

drawings by KATHERINE GRACE

published by CONSOLIDATED BOOK PUBLISHERS

Chicago 1, Illinois

contents

The editors and publishers wish to thank the American Dairy Association *for their kind permission to use the pie photograph on page 46.*

Copyright © 1958, THE HEARST CORPORATION

IN THE COLOR PHOTO ON THE FRONT COVER—Fresh Apple Pie, page 14. **ON THE BACK COVER**—Cutout Cherry Pie, page 16.

Tools for pretty pies: A pretty pie starts with the pastry. But unless you have the right tools, the job of blending and rolling out the dough can be difficult. At very little cost you can equip yourself with a big sifter, a blending fork or pastry blender, measuring cups for both liquid and dry ingredients, a spatula for leveling dry measurements, a pastry board or cloth, and a well-made rolling pin that spins at a touch, stockinet-covered if desired, a pastry wheel for cutting fluted strips, and cookie cutters for gay cutouts for pie tops. With these, any kind of pastry is easy to make, but a pie isn't a pie without a pie plate. Whether made of aluminum or oven glass, pie plates should be sturdy, well finished, easy to clean, and of a standard size: 8″, 9″ or 10″ wide, about 1¼″ deep.

Extra juicy pies: If yours run over, try these helps: Before baking, insert 1½″ pieces of uncooked macaroni in several vents; remove before serving. Wrap wet pie tape around rim before baking. Cut steam vents toward center, not near pie rim. Place foil, slightly larger than pie plate, on bottom rack of oven to catch juice; bake pie on upper rack; foil can be reused. Fluted or Fork Edge, page 12, helps hold in juices.

To avoid spilled fillings: Set partially filled custard or pumpkin pie on oven rack, then slowly pour in remaining filling. No spills!

If your pastry is tough: Perhaps you mixed it too long, handled it too strenuously, or used too much water. Good pastry takes speed, a light hand, little rolling. See recipes, pages 4 to 7.

If your pie shell buckles: You've added too few prebaking fork pricks on side and bottom, or failed to "peek" after 5 min. of baking to prick what blisters have appeared.

What to do with leftover pastry bits: Press pieces together; roll into ⅛″-thick sheet. Top with butter or margarine creamed with brown sugar and chopped nuts. Or use cinnamon mixed with sugar, or grated cheese. Cut pastry into strips, rounds, or squares. Or roll it up like a jelly roll; then slice ¼″ thick. Bake at 400°F. 8 to 10 min. Especially nice with tea, or for nibbling.

To help avoid weeping meringues: Never add more than 2 tablesp. sugar per egg white. And be sure to beat as our recipe on page 67 suggests. Always spread meringue from pastry rim in. Cool it slowly, away from drafts.

To store leftover fruit pies: Fruit pies are best when fresh; so, assuming what's left won't last longer than a day or so, cover well and store on pantry shelf. Freshen by warming a few minutes at 325°F. If you want to store pie in refrigerator, crust will taste better if pie is removed 20 min. before serving, then warmed at 325°F.

Food poisoning is no fun: Improperly stored pies have been known to cause it. Cream-filled pies cannot be left at room temperature. Refrigerate them immediately after they have cooled enough. Other pies that require constant refrigeration include all custard and gelatine variations, plus any involving whipped-cream topping or filling.

Cheese and pie: For downright good eating, nothing beats cheese with warm fruit pie. Try any of these favorites: sharp or mild Cheddar, whipped cream cheese, Swiss cheese, cheese food (handy rolls, individual wedges, etc.).

Alamode touch: A spoonful of ice cream is superb on warm fruit pie, perhaps with a sprinkle of nutmeg or cinnamon, too.

pastry & crusts

FLOUR 1 · SHORT ENING 2 · LIQUID 3

THE BIG 3
OF SUCCESSFUL PASTRY

Flour is the backbone of pastry. In these recipes, be sure to use *all-purpose flour* (family flour), sifting it just before making level measurements. All-purpose flour, with its gluten character, gives needed body to flaky, tender pastry.

Shortening makes pastry tender and flaky. *All-vegetable shortening* is creamy and bland in odor and taste. It blends quickly and easily, and lends tenderness and flakiness to pastry. Don't refrigerate —keep it on the pantry shelf. *Lard* is a traditional favorite for pastry. Regular lard must be refrigerated. New-type lard is stabilized in texture and flavor, so it need not be refrigerated. *Meat-and-vegetable shortening* is a blend of meat fats and vegetable oils—bland, creamy, excellent for pastry. It doesn't require refrigeration. *Salad oil*, a vegetable oil, is used as the shortening in our Stir-In Pastry, page 5, and No-Roll Pastry Shell, page 6.

Liquid binds and holds together the fat-and-flour particles. *Water* should be cold tap or boiling, as recipe specifies. *Milk* is sometimes used. The amount of liquid is very important. Too little makes dough break when rolled; too much toughens pastry. If recipe says "about," start with smaller amount, add more sparingly.

Flaky Tender Pastry

2¼ cups sifted all-purpose flour
1 teasp. salt
¾ cup plus 2 tablesp. shortening (except butter, margarine, or salad oil) at room temperature
About ⅓ cup cold tap water

1. Measure flour, salt, into sifter set in bowl; sift.
2. Cut two thirds of shortening into flour with pastry blender or 2 knives until like corn meal—for tenderness. Cut in remainder until like large peas—for flakiness. (Or cut in all at once until like coarse meal.)
3. Sprinkle water, 1 tablesp. at a time, over different parts of mixture, while tossing quickly with fork, until all particles stick together when pressed gently and form a dough that clings to fork around bowl.
4. Use only enough water to make flour particles cling together—they should not be wet or slippery. Amount may vary with flour.
5. Form pastry into smooth ball between cupped hands. Roll out at once (see pages 8 and 9). Or if it is a very warm day, wrap pastry in waxed paper or foil; refrigerate up to ½ hr.; then roll.

Makes 1 8″ or 9″ two-crust pie,
2 8″ or 9″ pie shells or one-crust pies,
or 8 to 10 3″ tart shells

Flaky Tender Pastry for One-Crust or Deep-Dish Pie: Use 1 cup plus 2 tablesp. flour, ½ teasp. salt, 7 tablesp. shortening, about 2 tablesp. plus 1 teasp. water.

Cheese Pastry: Add ½ to 1 cup grated process Cheddar cheese to flour after cutting in shortening.

P.S.—To freeze this pastry and the other pastries on these pages, see page 50.

Stir-In Pastry
(with salad oil)

2¼ cups sifted all-purpose flour
1½ teasp. salt
⅓ cup cold milk*
½ cup plus 1 tablesp. salad oil

1. Just before using pastry, make as follows: In bowl, mix flour, and salt. Pour milk and salad oil into same measuring cup (don't stir); add, *all at once*, to flour. With fork, stir lightly until well mixed.
2. With hands, press dough into smooth ball. Then divide in half; form into 2 balls.
3. Wipe table with damp cloth (so paper won't slip). Place half of pastry, flattened slightly, between 2 12″ square sheets of waxed paper. With rolling pin, roll out gently until pastry circle reaches edges of paper. Then peel off top sheet of paper. If pastry tears, mend by pressing edges together; or press piece of pastry lightly over tear; seal with fingers dipped in water.
4. Lift bottom sheet of paper and pastry by far corners (they will cling together). Place, with paper side up, in ungreased 8″ or 9″ pie plate. Carefully peel off paper. Gently ease and fit pastry into plate, as on pages 8 and 9.
5. Roll top crust in same way; lay over filling. Proceed as in step 9, page 9. Then cut 3 or 4 small slits near center, and bake as directed.

Makes 1 8″ or 9″ two-crust pie,
2 8″ or 9″ pie shells or one-crust pies,
or 8 to 10 3″ tart shells

*You can substitute ice water for milk. With fork, beat it with salad oil until thick and creamy. Immediately pour, *all at once*, over flour; then proceed as above.

Stir-In Pastry for One-Crust or Deep-Dish Pie: Use 1⅓ cups flour, 1 teasp. salt, ⅓ cup salad oil, 3 tablesp. milk or ice water.

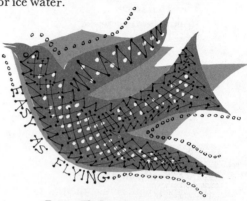

Easy Flaky Pastry

2¼ cups sifted all-purpose flour
1 teasp. salt
¾ cup shortening (except butter, margarine, or salad oil) at room temperature
5 tablesp. cold tap water

1. In bowl, mix flour and salt. With pastry blender or 2 knives, scissor-fashion, cut in shortening until size of peas.
2. Blend ⅓ cup flour-shortening mixture with water. Add to rest of flour mixture; with fork or fingers, mix until dough holds together.
3. Form pastry into smooth ball between cupped hands; roll out (see pages 8 and 9). Or if very warm day, wrap in waxed paper or foil; refrigerate up to ½ hr.; then roll.

Makes 1 8″ or 9″ two-crust pie,
2 8″ or 9″ pie shells or one-crust pies,
or 8 to 10 3″ tart shells

Easy Flaky Pastry for One-Crust or Deep-Dish Pie: Use 1½ cups flour, ½ teasp. salt, ½ cup shortening, 3 tablesp. water.

Water-Beat Pastry

¾ cup shortening (except butter,
   margarine, or salad oil) at room
   temperature
¼ cup boiling water
1 tablesp. milk
2 cups sifted all-purpose flour
1 teasp. salt

1. Put shortening in medium bowl. Add water, milk. Tilt bowl; then beat with silver fork in rapid cross-the-bowl strokes until mixture is smooth and thick—like whipped cream, and holds soft peaks when fork is lifted.
2. Sift flour, salt, onto shortening. Stir quickly, with round-the-bowl strokes, into dough that cleans bowl. Shape into smooth, flat round. Divide in half.
3. Roll on cloth-covered board (see page 3) or between squares of waxed paper, as in Stir-In Pastry, page 5.

   Makes 1 8″ or 9″ two-crust pie,
   2 8″ or 9″ pie shells or one-crust pies,
   or 8 to 10 3″ tart shells

Water-Beat Pastry for One-Crust or Deep-Dish Pie: Use ½ cup less 1 tablesp. shortening, 3 tablesp. boiling water, 1 teasp. milk, 1¼ cups flour, ½ teasp. salt.

No-Roll Pastry Shell

(with salad oil)

1½ cups sifted all-purpose flour
1½ teasp. sugar
1 teasp. salt
½ cup salad oil
2 tablesp. cold milk

Start heating oven to 425°F. Make pastry this easy way: Into 8″ pie plate, sift flour, sugar, salt. In measuring cup, combine oil, milk; with fork, beat; then pour, all at once, over flour mixture. With fork, mix until flour is completely dampened. With fingers, press pastry evenly and firmly to plate, to line bottom; then press pastry up side to line side and partly cover rim. Be sure pastry is uniform in thickness. To flute, pinch lightly with fingers. *Do not use a highly fluted edge.* Prick entire surface. Bake 12 to 15 min., or until golden.

Makes 1 8″ pie shell

Home Pastry Mix

6 cups sifted all-purpose flour
1 tablesp. salt
1 lb. shortening (except butter,
   margarine, or salad oil) at room
   temperature

Sift flour and salt into large bowl. Cut in shortening with pastry blender or 2 knives until like peas. Keep tightly covered on pantry shelf.   *Makes 9 cups*

To use: Sprinkle 3 cups of mix with 5 to 5½ tablesp. cold water, as in Flaky Tender Pastry, page 4.

Makes 1 8″ or 9″ two-crust pie,
2 8″ or 9″ pie shells or one-crust pies,
or 8 to 10 3″ tart shells

Packaged Piecrust Mix

You can now buy several brands of packaged piecrust mix with which you can make delicious pastry either right in the pie plate or in a mixing bowl. There are two reasons for the growing popularity of pie crust mix: The speed with which pastry can be made, and its uniform tenderness. Just add water or milk as label directs, mix quickly, and roll. You can use half of package, then store rest on pantry shelf for later use.

Makes 1 8″ or 9″ two-crust pie, or 2 8″ or 9″ pie shells or one-crust pies

To Make a Shapely Pie Shell

1. Prepare Packaged Piecrust Mix, on this page, or pastry for one-crust pie, pages 4–7.
2. Lightly roll out pastry ⅛″ thick (see To Make a Two-Crust Pie, page 9, steps 1–6).
3. Place loosely in pie plate; with hands or ball of pastry, pat out air so pastry fits snugly (*photo A*). Make stand-up rim (*photo B*) for Rope Edge, page 12; or make favorite edging, page 12.
4. *For unbaked pie shell:* If filling bakes in shell, *do not prick*. Fill, bake as directed. To pretty it up, see Pretty Pie Tops, page 66.
5. *For baked pie shell:* If shell is to be baked first, then filled, prick closely, deeply (*photo C*) with 4-tined fork on sides and bottom. Refrigerate ½ hr. Then bake at 450°F. 12 to 15 min.; or till golden. Peek after 5 min.; if bubbles appear, prick. Cool on rack.

Do ahead: Make pie shells, but don't bake; cover with waxed paper or foil; refrigerate 2 or 3 days if necessary; then bake. Or bake shells and store in covered container; reheat at 425°F. 5 min. See also Take Pie Shells, page 50.

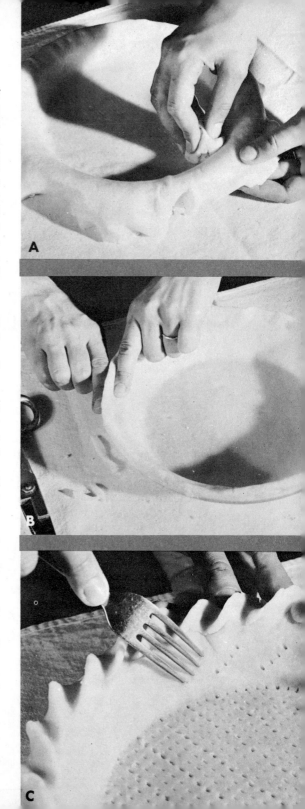

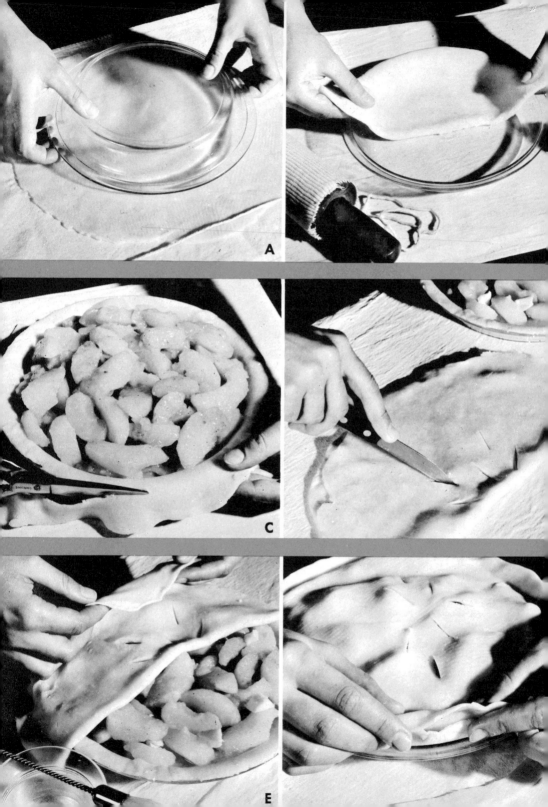

A

To Make a Two-Crust Pie

1. Prepare packaged piecrust mix, page 7, or make pastry for two-crust pie, pages 4–7.
2. Unless pastry recipe directs otherwise, lightly flour stockinet-covered rolling pin and cloth-covered board, or other plain surface (see page 3). Roll pin over cloth twice to rub in flour.
3. For bottom crust, lightly shape half of pastry into ball on cloth. Flatten, using light patting motions with rolling pin. Then make circle by rolling out lightly from center in all directions. As you approach edges, lift pin to keep them from splitting or getting thin. If they split, pinch together.
4. Lift pastry occasionally and give quarter turn, but do not turn it over. If it sticks, loosen gently with side of spatula, then lift and *lightly* flour board. *Remember that too much flour makes pastry tough.*
5. Continue rolling until circle is about 12″ in diameter (1½″ wider on all sides than inverted 8″ or 9″ pie plate, (*photo A*). Now fold it in half; lift onto ungreased plate, with fold at center (*photo B*); unfold. Using side of bent right index finger, or small ball of dough, gently fit pastry snugly to plate.
6. Be sure there are no cracks or small holes in pastry for filling or juice to seep through.
7. Fill lined pie plate. Trim bottom crust even with plate edge, using scissors (*photo C*).
8. For top crust, roll other half of pastry into 12″ circle. Fold in half; with knife, make slits (vents), below, near center fold so steam can escape (*photo D*), or make Cutout Vents, below. With fingers, moisten edge of lower crust with water (helps seal edges). Place top crust on filling, with fold at center; unfold (*photo E*). (Or roll circle of pastry over rolling pin; unroll into place over filled pie; then cut steam vents with knife.)
9. Trim top crust with scissors to ½″ overhang. Fold overhang under bottom crust; press together on edge (*photo F*). Finish with your favorite edging, page 12.
10. To insure a nice brown crust, glaze top of pie, page 66. Bake as recipe directs.

For extra-rich top crust: Roll out top crust into 12″ circle; dot with 2 tablesp. butter or margarine. Overlap pastry one way in thirds, then the other way in thirds. Roll out for top crust as in step 8. (Use Flaky Tender Pastry, page 4, or Easy Flaky Pastry, page 5, or Packaged Piecrust Mix, page 7.)

Steam Vents with Style

Fold 12″ pastry circle in half; at fold, with knife, cut one of green designs shown on this page; open on pie top.
Cutout Vents: Omit usual steam vents on top crust. Arrange top crust on pie.

With small shaped cutter—apple, heart, bunny, turkey, bell, etc.—make 5 or 6 cutouts all the way through top crust, but leaving cutouts in place. Glaze, page 66; bake.

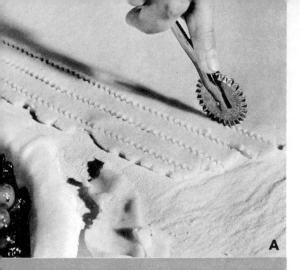

Trellis Pie

1. Line ungreased 9″ pie plate with pastry. Fill. Trim overhang to 1″. Roll pastry to 12″ circle; cut into ½″ strips with pastry wheel (*photo A*).
2. Moisten pastry edge with water; attach pastry strip to edge; press. Twist strip across filling; attach to pastry on opposite side; press firmly. Repeat with 4 strips, about 1¼″ apart (*photo B*). Repeat with 5 more strips crossing first ones (*photo C*).
3. Turn overhang up over rim and ends of trellis strips. With fingers, press firmly all around edge to seal.
4. Flute edge, see page 12, or press with floured fork. Brush edge and strips with cream or melted butter. Bake at 425°F. 40 to 50 min.

Single Trellis Pie: Make as Trellis Pie, placing 7 twisted strips only one way.
Lattice Pie: Make as Trellis Pie, leaving strips untwisted.

Unbaked Graham-Cracker Crust

Mix till crumbly 1⅓ cups graham-cracker crumbs, ⅓ cup brown sugar, ½ teasp. cinnamon, ⅓ cup melted butter or margarine. Set aside 3 tablesp. for pie top. With spoon, press rest to bottom and side of well-greased 9″ pie plate; *do not spread up on rim*. Refrigerate; fill as desired.

Nut Crust

Mix 1 cup finely ground Brazil nuts, pecans, walnuts, blanched almonds, or peanuts with 2 tablesp. granulated sugar. With back of spoon, press to bottom, side, of 9″ pie plate; *not on rim*. Bake at 400°F. about 8 min.

B

C

A

Baked Crumb Crusts

Follow these directions for any crust:

1. Let butter or margarine soften. Place a long length of waxed paper on pastry board; stack crackers, cookies, or pour cereal along center. Wrap, making double fold in paper; tuck ends under. Gently roll fine with rolling pin (*photo A*).
2. In 2-cup measuring cup, mix 1⅓ cups crumbs, sugar (if any) and butter with fork until crumbly (*photo B*). Set aside 3 tablesp. With back of spoon, press rest to bottom and sides of 9″ pie plate, forming small rim (*photo C*).
3. Bake at 375°F. 8 min. Cool; fill as desired; top with reserved crumbs.

Graham-Cracker Crust: Use 1⅓ cups graham cracker crumbs (about 16 crackers), ¼ cup butter or margarine, ¼ cup granulated sugar. *For 8″ Graham-Cracker Crust:* Use ¾ cup crumbs, 2 tablesp. butter or margarine, 2 tablesp. granulated sugar.

Vanilla Crumb Crust: Use 1⅓ cups vanilla wafer crumbs (about 24 2″ wafers), ¼ cup butter or margarine.

Chocolate Crumb Crust: Use 1⅓ cups chocolate wafer crumbs (about 18 2¾″ wafers), 3 tablesp. butter or margarine.

Gingersnap Crust: Use 1⅓ cups gingersnap crumbs (about 20 2″ cookies), 6 tablesp. butter or margarine.

Cereal-Flake Crust: Use 1⅓ cups cereal flake crumbs (about 3 cups corn or wheat flakes), ¼ cup butter or margarine, 2 tablesp. granulated sugar.

Nut-Crumb Crust: Use 1 cup crumbs; add ½ cup finely chopped walnuts, pecans, almonds or Brazil nuts.

Marble-Crumb Crust: Use 1 cup crumbs; add 2 sq. (2 oz.) unsweetened chocolate, grated.

A

B

C

edgings... try these
for pretty pies

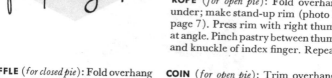

ROPE (*for open pie*): Fold overhang under; make stand-up rim (photo B, page 7). Press rim with right thumb at angle. Pinch pastry between thumb and knuckle of index finger. Repeat.

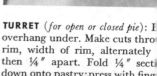
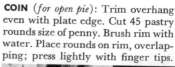

RUFFLE (*for closed pie*): Fold overhang under; make stand-up rim. Place left thumb and index finger ½" apart on rim. With right index finger pull pastry between fingers as shown.

COIN (*for open pie*): Trim overhang even with plate edge. Cut 45 pastry rounds size of penny. Brush rim with water. Place rounds on rim, overlapping; press lightly with finger tips.

TURRET (*for open or closed pie*): F overhang under. Make cuts thro rim, width of rim, alternately then ¼" apart. Fold ¼" secti down onto pastry; press with fing

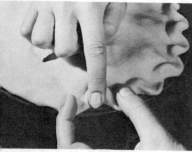

POLKA DOT (*for open or closed pie*): Fold overhang under. To shape, pat edge of pastry rim with thumb. With blunt end of floured wooden skewer, press even row of dots around rim.

FLUTED (*for open or closed pie*): Fold overhang under; make stand-up rim. Place right index finger on outside of rim; left thumb and index finger around pastry at that point. Pinch.

FORK (*for open or closed pie*): F overhang under; make stand-up ri With floured 4-tined fork, press pas to plate rim at ½" intervals. Or pr continuous row of fork marks on ri

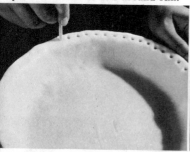

SCALLOPED (*for open or closed pie*): Fold overhang under; make edging as for Fluted edge, but leave ½" between points. Flatten points with floured 4-tined fork to form scallops.

TIERED (*for open pie*): Cut 8", 10", and 12" circles in 13" pastry round. Slit outer rings. Place 8" round in bottom of 9" plate; fit 12" ring to side; place 10" ring ¼" in from side.

BRAIDED (*for open pie*): Trim ove hang even with edge. Cut 9 past strips 14"x¼". Braid 3 strips; add braid. Repeat to make 30". Bru rim with water; press on braid edg

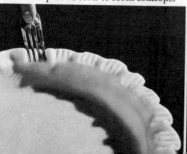

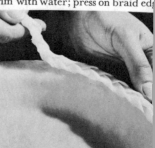

French Apple or Peach Pie

Make Fresh Apple Pie, page 14, or Golden Peach Pie, page 19, fluting bottom pastry crust, page 12, and using Crumbly Crust, below, for top crust. Bake as directed.

Serve as is or with whipped cream. Or mix confectioners' sugar with enough water to drizzle it on pie.

Crumbly Crust: Blend together with fork ½ cup brown sugar, firmly packed, ¼ cup butter or margarine, ⅓ cup sifted all-purpose flour, and ¼ teasp. cinnamon.

Coconut Apple Streusel: Make Fresh Apple Pie, page 14; omit top crust. Cover with 9″ pie plate; bake at 425°F. 20 min. Uncover; top with Crumbly Crust to which ½ cup each chopped nuts and flaked coconut are added; bake 20 min.

Mince-Apple Crumb Pie (*Pictured on pages 34 and 35*): Use 3 sliced, pared, cored apples; top with 2 cups prepared condensed or canned mincemeat, then Crumbly Crust.

Prize Prune Pie: Pit 2¾ cups cooked prunes. Arrange in unbaked 9″ pie shell, pages 4–7. Beat 1 egg with ⅓ cup granulated sugar, ⅛ teasp. salt, 1 tablesp. lemon juice, and ½ cup prune liquid. Pour over prunes. Sprinkle with Crumbly Crust; bake at 425°F. 40 min.

WILLIAM TELL

Elsie's Grated-Apple Pie

(*Pictured on pages 20 and 21*)

1 cup sifted all-purpose flour
½ teasp. baking powder
⅛ teasp. salt
¼ cup butter or margarine
2 tablesp. granulated sugar
1 egg
½ teasp. vanilla extract
4 pared large tart apples
2 tablesp. grated lemon rind
2 tablesp. lemon juice
1 cup granulated sugar
1 egg

Early in day: Start heating oven to 350°F. Into bowl, sift together flour, baking powder, and salt; with pastry blender or 2 knives, cut in butter until very fine. With fork, beat together 2 tablesp. sugar, 1 egg, and vanilla; stir into butter mixture. With fingers, press cookie-crust mixture to bottom and side of 9″ pie plate, and form small rim. Using fine grater, grate apples. Add lemon rind and juice, 1 cup sugar, and 1 egg; mix well. Turn into lined pie plate. Bake 50 to 60 min. Cool on wire rack. Top with 1 or more cheese cutouts (use cookie cutter and packaged process Cheddar cheese slices).

fruit & deep·dish pies

13

Fresh Apple Pie

(*Pictured on front cover*)

Pastry for 9″ two-crust pie, pages
4–7; or Cheese Pastry, page 4
1 to 2 teasp. lemon or pineapple
juice
1 to 2 tablesp. flour (if fruit is very
juicy)
⅔ to ¾ cup granulated sugar (or
half granulated, half brown)
¼ teasp. nutmeg
½ teasp. cinnamon
⅛ teasp. salt
½ teasp. grated lemon rind
6 to 7 cups thinly sliced, pared,
cored tart apples (2 lb. juicy
ones)*
1 tablesp. butter or margarine

Start heating oven to 425°F. Line 9″
pie plate with pastry as in To Make a
Two-Crust Pie, page 8 and 9. Combine
lemon juice with flour, sugar, nutmeg,
cinnamon, salt, lemon rind. (Amount of
sugar depends on tartness of apples.)
Place half of apples in plate, sharp edges
inward. Sprinkle with half of sugar mixture. Top with rest of apples, heaping
in center, then rest of sugar mixture.
Dot with butter; adjust top crust as
directed. Glaze, page 66. Bake 40 to
50 min., or until apples test tender with
fork and crust is brown.

Serve warm, as is; or top with vanilla
ice cream sprinkled with cinnamon,
cheese wedges, cream, whipped cream,
hard sauce, shaved maple sugar, sour
cream, or sharp-cheese spread.

*If apples are a nice red, try using
them unpared.

Apple Cream Pie: Before adjusting top
crust, pour ⅔ cup heavy cream, slightly
whipped, over apples. Luscious warm,
as is, or with individual wedges of sharp
Cheddar cheese.

Apple-Nut Pie: Add ½ cup chopped
nut meats to sugar.

Apple-Pineapple Pie: Substitute 1½
cups well-drained canned crushed pineapple for 1½ cups apple slices.

Better-Than-Ever Apple Pie: Make and
bake as Fresh Apple Pie, spreading 4
crushed, canned pear halves in bottom
of 9″ pastry-lined pie plate. Sprinkle
with 2 tablesp. white rum. Dice 4 to 5
pared tart apples; toss with ¾ to 1 cup
granulated sugar, ½ teasp. cinnamon,
2 tablesp. flour; heap over pears. Dot
with 2 tablesp. butter or margarine.

Holiday Apple Pie: Sprinkle 3 tablesp.
brandy through vents in crust when pie
is done.

Speedy Apple Pie: Delicious pie apples
—all pared, cored, sliced—come canned.
Make and bake in 8″ pie plate as Fresh
Apple Pie. For filling, use 1 No. 2 can
apples, ⅓ to ½ cup granulated sugar,
1 teasp. lemon juice, ¼ teasp. nutmeg,
dash salt, ¼ teasp. grated lemon rind,
¼ teasp. cinnamon, 1½ teasp. butter
or margarine. Add ½ to 1 tablesp.
flour unless you like it juicy.

Canned Berry or Fruit Pie: Make and
bake as Fresh Apple Pie, or Trellis Pie,
page 10. For filling, use 3 cups (2 No.
2½ cans or 3 No. 2 cans) drained
canned fruit (blueberries, blackberries,
raspberries, loganberries, boysenberries,
strawberries, peaches, plums, apricots),
½ to ¾ cup granulated sugar (depends
on sweetness of fruit), 3 tablesp. flour or
2 tablesp. quick-cooking tapioca, ½ cup
drained fruit juice, ½ teasp. nutmeg,
⅛ teasp. salt, ½ teasp. grated lemon
rind, ½ teasp. cinnamon, 1 tablesp.
butter or margarine.

Serve warm, with cheese, or top with
orange hard sauce, whipped cream,
vanilla ice cream, sour cream, or cream
cheese whipped with a little milk.

Fresh Berry or Fruit Pie (*Pictured on page 17, and pages 34 and 35*): Make and bake as Fresh Apple Pie, page 14; use 4 cups fruit, 2 tablesp. flour or 1½ tablesp. quick-cooking tapioca, 1 to 2 teasp. lemon juice, ⅔ to ¾ cup granulated sugar, ¼ teasp. nutmeg, ⅛ teasp. salt, ½ teasp. grated lemon rind, ½ teasp. cinnamon, 1 tablesp. butter or margarine.

Serve warm, as in Canned Berry or Fruit Pie, page 14.

Phyllis' Fresh Cherry Pie: Make pastry for 9″ two-crust pie, pages 4–7; line 9″ plate; make Rope Edge, page 12. Fill with 5 cups pitted, red, sour fresh cherries, 7 tablesp. flour, 1⅓ cups granulated sugar, ¼ teasp. almond extract, combined. Roll rest of pastry ⅛″ thick. Cut cherry leaf out of paper; use as pattern to cut 6 pastry "leaves." (Lightly trace veins with small spatula.) Arrange "leaves" on center of cherries in sunburst style. Brush "leaves" and edge with melted butter or margarine. Bake at 425°F. about 45 min., or until brown.

Serve warm, with vanilla ice cream.

Amber Pear Pie: Make and bake as Fresh Apple Pie, page 14. For filling, use 6 cups sliced pears, 1 to 2 teasp. lemon juice, ⅔ to ¾ cup granulated sugar, ½ teasp. nutmeg, ⅛ teasp. salt, ½ teasp. grated lemon rind, ½ teasp. cinnamon, 2 to 4 tablesp. flour, 1 tablesp. butter or margarine.

Serve warm, with vanilla ice cream sprinkled with a little nutmeg.

Rhubarb Pie: Make and bake as Fresh Apple Pie, page 14. For filling, use 4 cups rhubarb in 1″ pieces, 1½ cups granulated sugar, ¼ teasp. salt, 4 to 6 tablesp. flour or 2 to 4 tablesp. quick-cooking tapioca. Dot with 2 tablesp. butter or margarine. Or make as Trellis Pie, page 10. Or use frozen rhubarb, following directions on package.

Serve warm, delicious with cheese.

Rhubarb-Orange Pie: Add 2 tablesp. grated orange rind to Rhubarb Pie.

Strawberry-Rhubarb Pie (*Pictured on pages 20 and 21*): Make and bake as Fresh Apple Pie, page 14. For filling, use 3 cups each just-thawed frozen rhubarb and sliced fresh strawberries, ⅔ to ¾ cup granulated sugar, ½ teasp. nutmeg, ⅛ teasp. salt, ½ teasp. cinnamon, 3 to 4 tablesp. flour, 1 tablesp. butter or margarine. Or make as Trellis Pie, page 10.

JOHNNY APPLESEED

Superb Cheese-Apple Pie

Pastry for 9″ two-crust pie, pages 4–7
¾ cup granulated sugar
2 tablesp. flour
⅛ teasp. salt
1 cup grated process sharp Cheddar cheese
5 cups sliced, pared, cored apples
2 teasp. lemon juice
3 tablesp. heavy cream

Start heating oven to 425°F. Line 9″ pie plate with pastry; roll out top crust. Combine sugar, flour, salt, and ⅔ cup cheese. Sprinkle half of mixture in lined pie plate; heap apples on top; sprinkle with lemon juice. Cover with rest of sugar mixture, ⅓ cup cheese, and cream; adjust top crust. Bake 45 min., or until apples are tender. Serve warm.

Cutout Cherry Pie

(Pictured on back cover)

Pastry for 9″ two-crust pie, pages
    4–7
Cream
Cinnamon
Granulated sugar
1 cup granulated sugar
2 tablesp. quick-cooking tapioca
1 tablesp. cornstarch
¼ teasp. salt
2 No. 2 cans pitted red, sour
    cherries, packed in water
Red food color
¼ cup granulated sugar
½ teasp. almond extract

Early in day: Start heating oven to 450°F
Line 9″ pie plate with pastry; trim edge
even with pie plate. Roll out a bit more
pastry; with pastry wheel, cut out 4 or
5 ¾″-wide strips. Moisten one side of
pastry strips with water; then press
strips gently against inside edge of pastry
in pie plate, to make stand-up rim with
serrated edge. Roll out rest of dough;
using cardboard pattern, cut out 6
umbrellas with curved handles, making
each 3½″ long, 1″ wide, with handle
about 2½″ long. Place umbrellas on
baking sheet; brush with cream; sprinkle
lightly with mixture of cinnamon and
sugar; bake 5 min., or until golden
brown.

    In saucepan, mix together thoroughly
1 cup sugar, tapioca, cornstarch, and
salt. Drain canned cherries well, reserving 1 cup juice; add juice to sugar
mixture. Add red food color to mixture,
to make good red color. Cook over low
heat, stirring constantly, until clear and
thickened. Add well-drained cherries
and ¼ cup sugar; cook, stirring, 3 min.
longer; stir in extract. Pour into lined
pie plate.

Bake pie at 450°F. 10 min.; then reduce heat to 400°F. and bake 10 to 15
min. or until crust is brown and done.
Cool on wire rack about 1 hr.; then
arrange umbrellas on top, and finish
cooling. Pie will seem very juicy while
hot but thickens on cooling.

French Strawberry Pie

(Pictured on pages 34 and 35)

Mash 3 3-oz. pkgs. softened cream
cheese; beat smooth. Then spread in
baked 9″ pie shell, pages 4–7. Fill with
3 cups *well-drained* washed strawberries;
gently press to cheese. Melt ¾ cup currant or apple jelly over low heat; stir
smooth. Cool jelly, stirring occasionally;
spoon *cooled* jelly over berries. Refrigerate ½ hr., no longer.

Strawberry Triumph Pie

Baked 9″ pie shell, pages 4–7
1 qt. strawberries
1 cup granulated sugar
3 tablesp. cornstarch
2 tablesp. lemon juice
½ cup heavy cream, whipped

Wash berries; hull. Crush half of berries; stir in sugar, cornstarch, lemon
juice. Cook, stirring, over low heat till
thickened, transparent. Cool. Cut rest
of berries in half. Fold into cooked ones;
refrigerate in shell till set. Top with
cream.

IN THE COLOR PHOTO ON PAGE 17
—Fresh Blueberry Pie, page 15.

Spiced Peach Crunch Pie

(Pictured on page 45)

2 No. 2½ cans cling-peach slices
¼ cup chopped walnuts
1 pkg. piecrust mix
½ cup brown sugar, packed
½ teasp. cinnamon
1 tablesp. soft butter or margarine
1½ teasp. quick-cooking tapioca

1. Start heating oven to 425°F. Pour peaches into strainer or colander; drain *very well*. Chop nuts; with fork, mix with ½ pkg. piecrust mix, brown sugar, cinnamon, and butter until crumbly, with some large crumbs.
2. Prepare rest of piecrust mix, following directions on package for 1 pie shell. Roll out pastry; fit into 9″ pie plate, making attractive Fluted Edge, page 12.
3. In bottom of lined pie plate, arrange one third of peach slices, side by side, in ring; sprinkle with ½ teasp. tapioca. Repeat twice; sprinkle crumbly mixture evenly over top. Cover with foil; bake 30 min. Remove foil; bake 30 min. longer.

Makes 6 servings

Peach Meringue Pie

Ever tried peach pie with a meringue topping? Well do! It's good.

1 pkg. piecrust mix
1 tablesp. lemon juice
⅔ cup granulated sugar
⅛ teasp. salt
1 teasp. grated lemon rind
⅛ teasp. cinnamon
1½ to 2 tablesp. quick-cooking tapioca
4 cups sliced, peeled peaches
1 tablesp. butter or margarine
3-Egg-White Meringue, page 67

Prepare piecrust mix as package directs. Line 9″ pie plate, making Fluted Edge, page 12; refrigerate. Start heating oven to 425°F. Combine lemon juice, sugar, salt, grated lemon rind, cinnamon, and tapioca. (The amount of tapioca depends on the kind of pie you like—juicy or not so juicy—and we'll take ours juicy, using 1½ tablesp.)

Slice peaches. If very ripe, just rub back of knife over skins to loosen; peel off. Otherwise, place peaches in bowl, and cover with hot water a few minutes until skins loosen; then peel.

Quickly place half of sliced, peeled peaches in pastry-lined pie plate; sprinkle with half of sugar mixture. Top with rest of peaches; sprinkle with rest of sugar mixture. Dot with butter. Bake 35 min., or until peaches are just tender. Remove from oven. Turn oven heat down to 350°F.

Prepare meringue as directed. Pile on peaches, leaving surface irregular. Bake at 350°F 12 to 15 min. Remove from oven; cool on wire rack *away from drafts*. (Don't cool in refrigerator.)

Peach Glacé Pie

(Pictured on pages 34 and 35)

Baked 9″ pie shell, pages 4–7
1½ teasp. unflavored gelatine
2 tablesp. cold water
1 cup apricot preserves
¼ cup sherry
Pinch salt
1 No. 2½ can cling peach halves

Add gelatine to water; set aside. Bring preserves to boil. Remove; add gelatine; stir until melted. Add sherry, salt; cool until it begins to thicken. Pour into shell, over well-drained peaches, rounded sides up. Refrigerate till set.

Peach Crumble Pie

(Pictured on pages 20 and 21)

Unbaked 9″ pie shell, pages 4–7
2 No. 2½ cans cling-peach slices
2 tablesp. cornstarch
1 tablesp. grated lemon rind
2 tablesp. lemon juice
½ teasp. almond extract
Few drops yellow food color
  (optional)
¼ cup granulated sugar
¼ cup soft butter or margarine
1 cup crushed corn flakes

Early in day: Start heating oven to 450°F. Prick pie shell well; bake about 8 min., or until partly baked; remove to wire rack to cool a bit. Reduce oven temperature to 425°F.

Drain peaches well, reserving 1¼ cups syrup. In saucepan, stir reserved syrup into cornstarch until smooth. Cook, stirring, until clear and thickened. Add peach slices, lemon rind and juice, almond extract, and food color. Pour into partly baked pie shell. On top, with 2 forks or spoons, arrange some of the peach slices to form pin wheel.

To make crumbs: Combine sugar, butter, corn flakes until well mixed and crumbly; arrange around outer edge of pie, placing a few on center top. Bake at 425°F. about 20 min., or until crumbs are tinged with brown. Cool on wire rack.

BACCHUS

Golden Peach Pie

Pastry for 9″ two-crust pie, pages
  4–7
2½ cups cooked unsweetened
  dried peaches
½ cup peach liquid
1 tablesp. cornstarch
½ cup granulated sugar
Dash salt
¼ teasp. cinnamon
¼ teasp. nutmeg
2 tablesp. lemon juice
1 tablesp. butter or margarine

Make as Lattice Pie, page 10. For filling, arrange drained peaches in pastry-lined 9″ pie plate. Heat peach liquid; add cornstarch combined with sugar, salt, cinnamon, nutmeg; boil, stirring, until clear and thickened. Remove from heat; add lemon juice and butter. Pour mixture over peaches. Bake at 425°F. 40 min.

Prune-and-Apricot Pie: Stewed dried prunes and apricots, half and half, may replace peaches.

Aunt Jane's Grape Pie

Pastry for 9″ two-crust pie, pages
  4–7
4 cups stemmed Concord grapes
¾ cup granulated sugar
1½ tablesp. lemon juice
1 tablesp. grated orange rind
1 tablesp. quick-cooking tapioca

Make and bake as Fresh Apple Pie, page 14, or Trellis Pie, page 10. For filling, slip grapes out of skins; save skins. Cook pulp until seeds loosen; press through coarse sieve. Mix sieved pulp, skins, sugar, lemon juice, orange rind, and tapioca. Let stand 5 min. before using.

Cranberry Lattice Pie

Pastry for 9″ two-crust pie, pages 4–7
2 1-lb. cans whole-cranberry sauce
2 tablesp. butter or margarine
¼ cup brown sugar

Start heating oven to 425°F. Line 9″ pie plate with pastry. Roll out top crust; cut into strips for lattice top, page 10. Combine cranberry sauce, butter, and sugar; spoon into lined pie plate; arrange lattice crust on top, making Fluted Edge, page 12. Bake 30 to 40 min., or until golden. Serve warm, topped with vanilla cream.

Raisin Special Pie

(Pictured on pages 34 and 35)

Make and bake as 9″ Trellis Pie, page 10. For filling, combine 2 cups seedless raisins, 1 cup granulated sugar, 2 cups water, ½ teasp. salt, 2 tablesp. butter or margarine, 3 tablesp. lemon juice; boil 5 min. Stir in 2 tablesp. cornstarch mixed with 3 tablesp. water. Cook, stirring, 5 min. Add 1 teasp. lemon extract.

PIES IN THE COLOR PHOTO ON PAGES 20 AND 21—*On pedestals, left to right;* Berry Patch Parfait, page 39; Strawberry-Rhubarb, page 15; Fruit-Duet, page 22. *On pie rack, top to bottom:* Lime-Snow, page 27; Small Fry, page 63; Elsie's Grated Apple, page 13. *Second row:* Mocha Angel, page 62; Royal Chocolate Chiffon, page 36; Peach Crumble, page 19. *Front row:* Chocolate-Coconut Bavarian, page 32; Blueberry Cream, page 30; Wonderful Walnut, page 44; Lattice Coconut-Custard, page 43; Cranberry Fluff, page 40.

Epicure Apricot Pie

Baked 9″ pie shell, pages 4–7
1 3-oz. pkg. cream cheese
1 cup commercial sour cream
1 No. 2½ can apricot halves
⅓ cup granulated sugar
1 teasp. cinnamon

Blend cheese and sour cream until smooth.
About ½ hr. before serving: Spread cheese mixture in baked pie shell. Top with *well-drained* apricots. Sprinkle with combined sugar and cinnamon. Refrigerate.

Fruit-Duet Pie

(Pictured on pages 20 and 21)

2 cups dried apricots
1 tablesp. quick-cooking tapioca
1 cup granulated sugar
⅛ teasp. salt
Pastry for 9″ two-crust pie, pages 4–7
1 No. 2½ can pineapple chunks, drained
1 tablesp. grated lemon rind
1 tablesp. butter or margarine
Light cream

Night before: Pour 2 cups boiling water over apricots. Let soak overnight.
Early in day: Start heating oven to 450°F. Drain apricots, reserving ¼ cup juice. Combine this juice with tapioca, sugar, and salt; let stand 15 min. Meanwhile, line 9″ pie plate with pastry; roll out top crust. Combine apricots, pineapple, lemon rind, and tapioca mixture; toss together gently. Pour into lined pie plate; dot with butter. Adjust top crust; brush with cream. Bake at 450°F. 15 min.; then reduce oven temperature to 375°F., and bake 45 min. Cool on rack.

Mince Pie

Make and bake as Fresh Apple Pie, page 14, or Trellis Pie, page 10. To vary top crust, see page 66. For filling, use 3 cups prepared, packaged condensed or canned mincemeat.

Apple-Mince Pie: For filling, combine 2 cups pared, cored thin apple slices with 2 cups mincemeat.

Pineapple-Mince Pie: For filling, use 1 No. 2 can crushed pineapple, drained, spread over 2 cups mincemeat. Use Wagon Wheel, page 66, as top crust.

Walnut-Prune-Cot Pie

(Pictured on pages 34 and 35)

Bake 9″ pie shell, pages 4–7. Cook, sweeten, 1 lb. dried apricots and ½ lb. large dried prunes, as labels direct; drain. Put apricots in shell. Stuff pitted prunes with walnut halves or almonds; set around edge. Warm up ¼ cup white corn syrup with ¼ teasp. cinnamon, 1 teasp. grated lemon rind; drizzle mixture on fruit.

To serve: Cut pie in wedges; top with custard sauce.

Envelope Pie

(Pictured on page 45)

2 teasp. grated orange rind
½ cup brown sugar, packed
1 teasp. cinnamon
½ cup grated process sharp Cheddar cheese
1 pkg. piecrust mix
6 pared, cored pear halves
Light cream

1. Start heating oven to 425°F. Mix grated orange rind with sugar, cinnamon.

2. Add cheese to piecrust mix; mix as label directs. Place pastry on 17″x14″ baking sheet. With narrow end of baking sheet facing you, roll out pastry to fit baking sheet.

3. On lower half of pastry, arrange pears crosswise; sprinkle with sugar mixture. Bring top half of pastry over pears, loosening pastry with spatula if needed.

4. With fork, press together to seal. Prick top. Bake 30 min. Serve with cream, sweetened and sprinkled with nutmeg.   *Makes 6 servings*

Green-Tomato Pie

Pastry for 8″ two-crust pie, pages 4–7; or 1 pkg. piecrust mix
6 medium green tomatoes
1 cup granulated sugar
1 teasp. salt
½ teasp. cinnamon
2 tablesp. flour
½ teasp. nutmeg
3 tablesp. lemon juice
1 teasp. grated lemon rind
1 tablesp. butter or margarine

1. Start heating oven to 425°F. Roll out half of pastry as recipe or label directs; fit to 8″ pie plate.

2. Core, thinly slice, then quarter tomatoes (you'll need 3 to 4 cups).

3. Combine sugar, salt, cinnamon, flour, nutmeg; add to tomatoes; toss lightly. Add lemon juice, rind.

4. Turn tomato mixture into pastry-lined pie plate; dot with butter. Roll out rest of pastry for top crust; place on pie; seal and flute edges, page 12; cut slits in top.

5. Bake pie 40 to 45 min., or until tomatoes are tender. Serve slightly warm.

Apple Deep-Dish Pie

Pastry for deep-dish pie, pages 4–7
¾ to 1 cup granulated sugar (or part brown)
2 tablesp. flour
⅛ teasp. salt
¼ teasp. nutmeg
¼ teasp. cinnamon
1 teasp. lemon juice
2 teasp. butter or margarine
6 cups pared, cored tart apple slices, ¼″ thick

Start heating oven to 425°F. Combine sugar, flour, salt, nutmeg, cinnamon, lemon juice, and butter. Arrange apples in 10″x6″x2″ (1½-qt.) baking dish; sprinkle with sugar mixture. Roll pastry to fit top of dish with ½″ overhang; cut several small slits for steam vents or make Cutout Vents, page 9. Lay pastry loosely over apples; fold overhang under; press onto rim firmly with upturned tines of floured fork. Glaze, page 66. Bake 40 min., or until apples are done.
Makes 6 servings

A new twist: Make ½ recipe for Cheese Pastry, page 4, for top crust. Or top apples with ½ cup currants, raisins, chopped nuts, date slices, or flaked coconut, or 8 large marshmallows, before adjusting top crust.

Raspberry or Fresh Peach Deep-Dish Pie: (*Pictured on pages 34 and 35*): For filling, use ⅔ to ¾ cup granulated sugar, 3 tablesp. flour, ⅛ teasp. salt, ¼ teasp. nutmeg, ¼ teasp. cinnamon, 1 teasp. lemon juice, 2 teasp. butter, 4 cups raspberries or sliced, peeled peaches.

Strawberry-Rhubarb Deep-Dish Pie

(*Pictured on pages 34 and 35*)

Make Strawberry-Rhubarb Pie, page 15, in 10″x6″x2″ baking dish, with lattice top, page 10. Bake at 425°F. 40 min.
Makes 6 servings

Aunt Jane's Grape Deep-Dish Pie

Start heating oven to 425°F. Make twice filling for Aunt Jane's Grape Pie, page 19, in 9″x9″x2″ (2-qt.) baking dish. For top, roll pastry for deep-dish pie, pages 4–7, 1″ larger than top of dish; from center cut out a grape cluster, using thimble. Place pastry over grape mixture; press overhang firmly to edge. Cut 1″-wide pastry strips; place around edge of pie; seal to edge. Mark pastry edge, ½″ apart, with dull edge of knife. Cut out 3 pastry leaves; arrange in corner at stem end of grape cluster. Bake 40 min. *Makes 8 servings*

IN THE COLOR PHOTO ON PAGE 24
—Lemon Meringue Pie, page 27, and lemon meringue tarts.

Plum Deep-Dish Pie

Pastry for deep-dish pie, pages 4–7
1¼ cups granulated sugar
3 tablesp. flour
⅛ teasp. salt
¼ teasp. almond extract
2 tablesp. butter or margarine
4 cups halved, pitted plums (about 2½ lb.)

Start heating oven to 425°F. For filling, combine sugar, flour, salt, extract, butter. Arrange plums in 10"x6"x2" baking dish; sprinkle with sugar mixture. Adjust top crust as in Apple Deep-Dish Pie, page 25. Glaze, page 66. Bake 45 to 50 min. *Makes 6 servings*

Winter Plum Deep-Dish Pie: For filling, use ½ cup sugar, 3 tablesp. flour, ¼ teasp. salt, ¼ teasp. almond extract, 2 tablesp. butter or margarine, 4 cups drained canned pitted plums (2 No. 2½ cans), ½ cup plum juice, 2 tablesp. lemon juice.

Red Cherry Deep-Dish Pie: For filling, use 2 cups sugar, 6 tablesp. flour, ⅛ teasp. salt, ¼ teasp. almond extract, 2 tablesp. butter or margarine, 4 cups drained, canned, sour red pitted cherries (2 No. 2 cans), ½ cup cherry juice.

Apricot Basket Weave Deep-Dish Pie: Make in 9" round baking dish, using ½ cup sugar, 4 tablesp. flour, ½ teasp. salt, ¼ teasp. almond extract, 2 tablesp. butter, 4 cups drained, canned apricot halves (2 No. 2½ cans), ½ cup apricot juice, 1 tablesp. lemon juice, as filling.

Roll half of pastry *very* thin on waxed paper; cut in 1"-wide strips. Roll other half on more waxed paper; cut in 1"-wide strips: weave in and out of first strips. Lay paper side up, on top; peel off paper; press strips to rim; trim even. Roll trimmings thin; cut in 1"-wide strips; place around edge of pie; press.

Deep-Dish Golden Mince Pie

Perfect climax to any Christmas dinner— or it can go right into the freezer and wait for a postholiday party. Wrap in freezer wrap, and tie with ribbon.

Start heating oven to 425°F. Arrange contents of 2 1-lb. 7-oz. cans mincemeat (or 2 9-oz. pkgs. condensed mincemeat, prepared), and ½ orange, *thinly sliced*, in 12"x8"x2" baking dish. Roll pastry for deep-dish pie, pages 4–7, to fit top of dish, with ½" overhang; lay loosely over mincemeat; fold overhang under; press onto rim firmly, fluting pastry edge, page 12. Brush with light cream; bake 30 min. Roll out remaining dough ⅛" thick; cut out with small reindeer cookie cutter. (If freezing for future use, use any shape cookie cutter desired.) Place reindeer cutouts on ungreased baking sheet. Bake 10 to 12 min. "Glue" onto crust with mixture of little confectioners' sugar and water.

Toppings For Deep-Dish Pies

Any of these are delicious on a warm deep-dish pie:

Pour cream or ice cream, with dash of nutmeg or mace
Whipped cream, topped with brown sugar and nutmeg, cinnamon and sugar, chopped nuts, or grated orange rind
Hard sauce, with rum extract, chopped nuts, or raisins folded in
Cream or cottage cheese, with bit of grated orange rind folded in

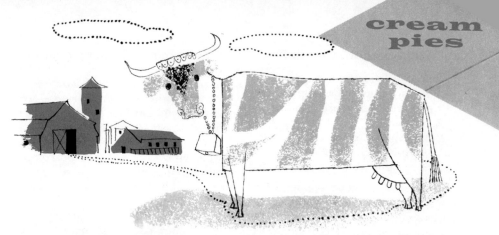

Lemon Meringue Pie

(Pictured on page 24)

Baked 9″ pie shell, pages 4–7; or
   Baked Crumb Crust, page 11
¾ cup granulated sugar
7 tablesp. all-purpose flour
2 tablesp. cornstarch
½ teasp. salt
2¼ cups boiling water
3 egg yolks
¼ cup granulated sugar
6 tablesp. lemon juice
3 tablesp. grated lemon rind
3-Egg-White Meringue, page 67

In double boiler, combine ¾ cup sugar with flour, cornstarch, and salt. Slowly stir in boiling water. Cook over boiling water until smooth and *just* thick enough to mound (for a pie a bit on the runny side). For a thicker pie, cook until mound is firmer. Beat yolks with ¼ cup sugar; slowly stir into hot filling. Blend well. Return to double boiler; cook 5 min. over boiling water, stirring occasionally. Add lemon juice, rind. Remove at once; cool; pour into shell. Top with meringue. Bake as directed. Serve any leftover pie in sherbet glasses—crust and all.

To vary: Top meringue with flaked coconut, slivered almonds, or miniature marshmallows before baking. Or omit meringue; top with whipped cream.

Lemon-Snow Pie: Increase flour to ½ cup. Fold meringue into cooled filling. Turn into baked shell. Chill. Top with strawberries if desired.

Lime Meringue Pie *(Pictured on pages 34 and 35)*: Substitute lime rind and juice for lemon. Add drop each green and yellow food color.

Lime-Snow Pie *(Pictured on pages 20 and 21)*: Make as Lime Meringue Pie, folding meringue into cooled filling. Turn into baked pie shell. Refrigerate at least 5 hrs. before serving. If desired, garnish with a few raspberries.

Orange-Coconut Pie: Substitute orange rind and juice for lemon. Reduce ¾ cup sugar to ⅔ cup; add ½ cup flaked coconut. Top meringue with ¼ cup coconut; bake.

Pineapple Meringue Pie: Reduce lemon juice to 2 tablesp. Reduce ¾ cup sugar to ⅔ cup. Add ⅔ cup well-drained, canned crushed pineapple to hot filling.

Pineapple-Snow Pie: Make Pineapple Meringue Pie with these changes: Into cooled filling, fold meringue as well as the crushed pineapple.

Quick Lemon Pie: Use packaged lemon-pie filling; add to hot filling 1 tablesp. each butter and grated lemon rind.

Satin-Smooth Cream Pie

Baked 9″ pie shell, pages 4–7; or
  Baked Crumb Crust, page 11
1 pkg. regular vanilla pudding
2 cups milk
2 tablesp. butter or margarine
¼ teasp. vanilla or almond extract
½–⅔ cup heavy cream, whipped

(If you want meringue topping, see below.) Prepare pudding as directed on package, using 2 cups milk; add butter, extract. Cover surface of pudding with waxed paper; refrigerate. Beat with spoon till smooth; spoon into baked pie shell; refrigerate. Top with whipped cream; serve. Or top whipped cream with any one of these:

  Grated chocolate or orange rind, chopped nuts, cinnamon or nutmeg
  Well-drained, canned crushed pineapple or sliced peaches; orange sections; strawberries or raspberries
  Sliced bananas or peaches; toasted, fresh or flaked coconut
  Crushed peanut brittle; chopped chocolate mints
  Substitute marshmallow cream for whipped cream; top with coconut
  Add 1½ teasp. instant coffee or cocoa to cream while whipping

Meringue-Topped Cream Pie: Omit whipped cream. Add 2 egg yolks to milk. Top with 2-Egg-White Meringue, page 67. Sprinkle with flaked coconut or chopped nuts before baking. Or spread cream filling with 1 cup sieved, stewed apricots before topping.

De Luxe Cream Pie: Reduce milk to 1½ cups; fold whipped cream into beaten cold filling.

Banana Cream Pie: Arrange ½″ layer of sliced bananas in shell just before filling. Top with whipped cream; circle with banana slices dipped in citrus-fruit juice, and toasted coconut if desired. To vary, substitute lemon or rum extract.

Coconut Cream Pie: Fold ½ to 1 cup flaked, toasted, or grated fresh coconut into hot filling. Garnish top with whipped cream, then ¼ cup coconut; or whipped cream, fruit, and coconut. Or garnish with meringue and coconut before baking.

Note: Packaged coconut-cream-pudding, butterscotch pudding, and chocolate pudding make delicious cream pies too. Follow label directions.

Butterscotch Cream Pie

Baked 9″ pie shell, pages 4–7
½ cup light brown sugar, packed
⅓ cup all-purpose flour
¼ teasp. salt
2 cups milk
3 egg yolks
¼ cup light brown sugar, packed
3 tablesp. butter or margarine
1 teasp. vanilla extract
3 Egg-White Meringue, page 67*

In double boiler, combine ½ cup brown sugar, flour, salt; gradually stir in milk; cook, stirring until thick; then cook, covered, stirring occasionally, 10 min. longer. Beat egg yolks with ¼ cup brown sugar; stir in a little sauce; add to rest of sauce in double boiler. Cook, stirring, 2 min. or until mixture mounds when dropped from spoon. Add butter, vanilla, cool. Start heating oven to 350°F. Turn filling into pie shell. Cover with meringue; bake 12 to 15 min.

Makes 1 9″ pie

*Or omit meringue. Top pie with ½ cup heavy cream, whipped; sprinkle with shaved chocolate.

Chocolate Cream Pie: Substitute ¼ cup granulated sugar for ½ cup light brown sugar, and ¼ cup granulated sugar for ¼ cup brown sugar. To flour-sugar mixture in double boiler add 2 to 2½ sq. unsweetened chocolate, cut up. When chocolate is melted, beat smooth with egg beater. Nice topped with sliced bananas.

Double Cream Pie
(*Pictured on page 45*)

1 pkg. piecrust mix
1 pkg. regular chocolate pudding
1 pkg. regular vanilla pudding
3 cups milk
¼ teasp. almond extract
1 cup heavy cream, whipped
Flaked coconut

1. Prepare 1 baked 9″ pie shell as directed on piecrust-mix package.
2. Prepare chocolate, then vanilla, pudding as label directs, using 1½ cups milk for each. Cover surface of puddings with waxed paper; refrigerate till cold. Then, into vanilla pudding, fold almond extract and half of cream; fold rest of cream into chocolate pudding.
3. Using 17″-long piece of foil, make collar, 4½″ in diameter and about 3″ high. Set in center of baked pie shell. Spoon chocolate mixture into center, vanilla around outside (spoon any leftover pudding into custard cups). Carefully lift out foil collar.
4. Refrigerate several hours. Garnish vanilla pudding with coconut.

Makes 8 servings

So Easy Banana-Caramel Pie

Baked 8″ pie shell, pages 4–7
¼ cup cold water
2 egg yolks
½ cup granulated sugar
½ cup brown sugar, packed
¼ cup all-purpose flour
¼ teasp. salt
1 cup boiling water
1 tablesp. butter or margarine
½ teasp. vanilla extract
3 or 4 ripe bananas
½ cup heavy cream

Early in day: In saucepan, mix cold water with egg yolks; stir in combined sugars, flour, and salt. Gradually add boiling water, stirring briskly. Cook, stirring, 3 to 5 min., or until smooth and thick. Add butter and vanilla; cool 5 min., stirring occasionally. Pour into baked pie shell. Refrigerate till serving time.

To serve: Slice bananas; brush with lemon juice; arrange over filling. Whip cream; spread over all.

Picture Peach Cream Pie

Pretty as a picture, and tasty, too!

Add 1 teasp. unflavored gelatine to 1 pkg. regular vanilla pudding; then prepare by label directions, using 1½ cups milk to which 2 egg yolks are added and blended. Cool; fold in ⅓ cup heavy cream, whipped, ¼ teasp. almond extract. Place 3 to 4 sliced peaches, brushed with lemon juice, or 1 No. 2½ can drained sliced peaches, or 2 pkg. drained, thawed, frozen peaches in baked 9″ pie shell, pages 4–7, (save a few for top). Spoon on filling; refrigerate. Top with Meringue Crown, page 67, then peaches.

Blueberry Cream Pie

(Pictured on pages 20 and 21)

Baked 8″ pie shell, pages 4–7
1 pkg. regular vanilla pudding
1½ cups milk
½ cup heavy cream, whipped
1 pkg. (2 cups) thawed frozen
    unsweetened blueberries; or
    2 cups fresh blueberries
1 tablesp. cornstarch
2 tablesp. granulated sugar
1 tablesp. grated lemon rind
1 tablesp. lemon juice

Early in day: Make pudding as package directs, using 1½ cups milk; refrigerate until cold. Fold in whipped cream; turn into baked pie shell. Refrigerate until firm. Meanwhile, make Blueberry Topping: In saucepan, place scant 1 cup blueberries; add combined cornstarch and sugar, lemon rind and juice. Cook over low heat, mashing and stirring, until mixture thickens and clears. Add rest of berries; cool slightly; then carefully spoon over pudding in pie shell. Refrigerate until serving time.

Pineapple Cream Pie: For Blueberry Topping substitute following: Combine 1 cup drained canned crushed pineapple with 2 tablesp. juice from pineapple, 1½ teasp. cornstarch, 1 tablesp. granulated sugar, 1½ teasp. grated lemon rind, and 1½ teasp. lemon juice. Cook over low heat, stirring, until thick and clear; cool slightly.

Cranberry Cream Pie: For Blueberry Topping substitute following: Combine 1 cup canned whole-cranberry sauce with 1½ teasp. cornstarch, 1 tablesp. granulated sugar, 1½ teasp. grated lemon rind, and 1½ teasp. lemon juice. Cook over low heat, stirring, until thick and clear; cool slightly. Nice for that turkey dinner.

Butterscotch-Date Cream Pie

Baked 9″ pie shell, pages 4–7
2½ cups milk, diluted evaporated
    milk, or liquefied nonfat dry milk
6 tablesp. butter or margarine
2 egg yolks
1 cup light-brown sugar, packed
¼ cup cornstarch
Dash salt
½ cup sliced, pitted dates
1 teasp. vanilla extract
1 cup heavy cream, whipped
¼ cup chopped pecans

Early in day: In double boiler, heat 2 cups milk with butter. Beat yolks; stir in combined sugar, cornstarch, and salt; blend in remaining ½ cup milk; add to heated milk in double boiler. Cook over hot, *not boiling*, water, stirring, until thick and smooth. Add dates and vanilla. Refrigerate till cold. Then turn into baked pie shell; refrigerate at least 6 hrs., or until set.

To serve: Garnish pie with whipped cream, making swirls, then sprinkle chopped pecans around inside of rim.

Rhubarb Cream Pie

Make and bake as Trellis Pie, page 10. For filling, blend 1½ cups granulated sugar, 3 tablesp. flour, ½ teasp. nutmeg, 1 tablesp. butter or margarine; add 2 well-beaten eggs, 3 cups rhubarb cut in 1″ pieces.

Susan's Heavenly Pie

1½ cups granulated sugar
¼ teasp. cream of tartar
4 egg whites
3 tablesp. flaked coconut
  (optional)
4 egg yolks
3 tablesp. lemon juice
1 tablesp. grated lemon rind
⅛ teasp. salt
1 pt. heavy cream
Strawberries

1. Start heating oven to 275°F. *For Meringue Crust:* Sift 1 cup sugar with cream of tartar. Beat egg whites (with hand or electric beater) till they stand in stiff, not dry, peaks. Slowly add sugar, beating.

2. When meringue makes very stiff, glossy peaks, spread over bottom, up side, just to rim, of well-greased 9" pie plate, making bottom ¼" thick, side 1" thick. Sprinkle rim with 2 tablesp. coconut. Bake 1 hr., or until light brown and crisp. Cool.

3. Beat egg yolks slightly in double-boiler top; stir in ½ cup sugar, lemon juice, lemon rind, salt. Cook, stirring, over boiling water till thick —about 8 to 10 min. Cool. Whip 1 cup cream. Fold custard into it.

4. Slowly pour cool lemon-cream into center of cooled, baked meringue shell, making sure all pockets are full. Smooth top.

5. Refrigerate 12 to 24 hrs. to mellow meringue and filling. This makes cutting neat wedges no trick at all.

6. To serve, top with 1 cup cream, whipped, and sprinkle with 1 tablesp. coconut, toasted. Garnish with strawberries.

Heavenly Apricot-Cream Pie: Make and bake Meringue Crust as above. For filling, drain well and purée canned apricots (or use baby food); fold 1 cup purée into 1 cup heavy cream, whipped. Spread in baked meringue shell. Top with thick layer of toasted coconut.

Easy Heavenly Pie: Make and bake Meringue Crust as above. For filling, make up half a package of lemon-pie filling, adding 1 tablesp. butter and 2 teasp. grated lemon rind. Cool. Pour into baked meringue shell. Refrigerate. Top with whipped cream and strawberries, if desired.

Heavenly Coffee Pie: Make and bake Meringue Crust as above. Flavor heavy cream with instant coffee; whip. Sweeten to taste. Fill shell.

Mile-High Fig Pie

Baked 8" pie shell, pages 4–7
1 cup dried figs
3 egg yolks
½ cup commercial sour cream
¼ cup lemon juice
Pinch salt
½ cup granulated sugar
½ cup coarsely chopped walnuts
1 teasp. vanilla extract
1 tablesp. grated lemon rind
3-Egg-White Meringue, page 67

Early in day: Pour boiling water over figs; let stand 5 min.; drain. With scissors, snip off stems; then coarsely snip up figs. In saucepan, beat egg yolks slightly; stir in figs, sour cream, lemon juice, salt, and ½ cup sugar. Bring to boil over low heat, stirring; then boil, stirring, 3 min. Refrigerate until cool and stiff. Start heating oven to 350°F. Into fig mixture, stir nuts, vanilla, lemon rind; pour into pie shell. Top with meringue. Bake 12 to 15 min.; cool away from drafts.

Lime-Swirl Chiffon Pie: Omit the ⅓ cup sugar. Substitute lime juice for lemon, 1 teasp. grated lime rind for lemon. Swirl whipped cream through filling in shell. Top with ½ teasp. grated lime rind.

Orange Chiffon Pie: Reduce lemon juice to 1 tablesp.; to juice add ¼ cup thawed frozen orange-juice concentrate. Reduce ½ cup sugar, beaten with whites, to ⅓ cup.

Chocolate-Coconut Bavarian Pie

(Pictured on pages 20 and 21)

2 sq. unsweetened chocolate
2 tablesp. butter or margarine
2 tablesp. hot milk or water
⅔ cup sifted confectioners' sugar
1½ cups snipped flaked coconut
1 env. unflavored gelatine
¼ cup granulated sugar
3 egg yolks
1¼ cups milk
3 egg whites
¼ teasp. salt
¼ cup granulated sugar
1 cup heavy cream, whipped
1 teasp. vanilla extract
1 cup flaked coconut
1 sq. unsweetened chocolate, grated

Early in day: For Chocolate Coconut Crust: Grease 8″ pie plate. In double boiler, melt 2 sq. chocolate and butter; stir to blend. Combine hot milk, confectioners' sugar: stir into chocolate mixture. Add 1½ cups coconut; mix well. Press to bottom, side, of pie plate. Refrigerate.

For filling, combine gelatine with ¼ cup granulated sugar. In double-boiler top, beat yolks; stir in gelatine mixture and milk. Cook over hot, *not boiling*, water, stirring, until custard coats

Lemon Chiffon Pie

Baked 9″ pie shell, pages 4–7;
   or Baked Crumb Crust, page 11;
   or Unbaked Graham-Cracker
   Crust, page 11
1½ teasp. unflavored gelatine
⅓ cup granulated sugar
4 egg yolks
1 tablesp. grated lemon rind
¼ cup lemon juice
⅓ cup cold water
4 egg whites
¼ teasp. salt
½ cup granulated sugar
½ cup heavy cream, whipped

Add gelatine to ⅓ cup sugar. Put yolks in double boiler; stir in lemon rind and juice, water, then gelatine mixture. Cook, stirring, over boiling water 5 min., or till thickened. *Remove from heat.* Beat egg whites and salt till they form peaks when beater is raised. Slowly add ½ cup sugar, while beating stiff. Gently fold in hot mixture. Turn into shell; refrigerate till set.

To serve: Spread cream on pie. May be topped with blueberries or sliced strawberries or bananas.

spoon. Refrigerate, stirring occasionally, until custard mounds when dropped from spoon; then beat just until smooth. Beat egg whites with salt till quite stiff; gradually add ¼ cup granulated sugar, beating until stiff; fold in custard mixture, then whipped cream, vanilla, ½ cup coconut. Pour into crust, reserving about one third of mixture. Refrigerate pie and reserved filling until almost set; then heap remaining filling on center top of pie; refrigerate until serving time.

About 15 min. before serving: Remove pie from refrigerator. Garnish top with combined ½ cup coconut and grated chocolate.

To vary: Refrigerate crust until firm; to serve, heap with favorite ice cream.

Californian Lemon-Puff Pie

Baked 9″ pie shell, pages 4–7
4 egg yolks
¼ cup granulated sugar
1 teasp. grated lemon rind
¼ cup lemon juice
4 egg whites
Dash salt
½ cup granulated sugar

Start heating oven to 325°F. Cook yolks, ¼ cup sugar, lemon rind and lemon juice, in double boiler, stirring, till thickened. Beat whites with salt till stiff, not dry; slowly beat in ½ cup sugar; beat stiff. Fold into hot mixture; heap in shell. Bake 15 to 20 min., or till golden. Cool. (It settles a bit.)

Chocolate Chiffon Pie

1. Soak 1 env. unflavored gelatine in ¼ cup water. In double boiler melt 2 sq. unsweetened chocolate in ½ cup water; stir into 3 egg yolks.
2. Return to double boiler; cook, stirring, till creamy (about 2 min.). Stir in gelatine until dissolved; pour into bowl.
3. Add ¼ teasp. salt, 1 teasp. vanilla extract; stir. Beat 3 egg whites till they peak when beater is raised. Slowly beat in ½ cup granulated sugar. Fold into chocolate (*photo A*).
4. Spoon into Baked Crumb Crust, page 11; refrigerate until set. To serve, top with ½ cup heavy cream, whipped; sprinkle with reserved crumbs (*photo B*).

To vary: Top with chopped salted nuts. Or add 2 teasp. instant coffee or rum to cream before whipping.

Rocky-Road Chiffon Pie: Add 6 to 8 quartered large marshmallows, ½ cup chopped nuts, to filling with meringue.

Royal Chocolate Chiffon Pie

(Pictured on pages 20 and 21)

Baked 9″ pie shell, pages 4–7
1 env. unflavored gelatine
¾ cup granulated sugar
⅛ teasp. salt
1 egg yolk
¾ cup milk
3 sq. unsweetened chocolate
1 cup undiluted evaporated milk
1 teasp. vanilla extract
1 cup heavy cream
1 sq. unsweetened chocolate

Day before or early in day: Combine gelatine, sugar, and salt. In double-boiler top, beat egg yolk; stir in milk, then gelatine mixture; add 3 sq. chocolate. Cook over boiling water, stirring, until chocolate is melted. Remove from heat; with egg beater, beat until smooth. Refrigerate, stirring occasionally, until mixture mounds when dropped from spoon. Store evaporated milk in ice-cube tray of refrigerator until soft ice crystals form around edges—15 to 20 min.; beat until stiff; fold in chocolate mixture and vanilla. Turn into baked pie shell. Refrigerate until set.

PIES IN THE COLOR PHOTO ON PAGES 34 AND 35—*Front row, left to right:* Fresh Fruit, page 15; Strawberry-Rhubarb Deep-Dish, page 25. *Second row:* Chocolate Mousse, page 63; Mince-Apple Crumb, page 13; Cranberry Fluff, page 40; Peach Glacé, page 18; Raisin Special, page 22; Pineapple-Cheese, page 47; Coffee Velvet, page 37. *Third row:* Coconut Custard, page 43; Down-South Pecan, page 44; Walnut-Prune-Cot, page 23; Candy Velvet, page 37; French Strawberry, page 16; Lime Meringue, page 27; Fudge-Nut, page 44. *Fourth row:* Butterscotch-Banana Cream Tarts, page 58; Lemon Cream Shortcake Tarts, page 58; Baked Open Pumpkin Tarts, page 55; Raspberry Deep-Dish, page 25; Cream-Cheese Turnovers, page 61. *Top row:* Apple Pielets, page 55; Satin-Smooth Cream Tarts, page 58.

To serve: Whip heavy cream; sweeten a bit if desired; pile in center of pie, and spread out somewhat as shown in photo. Shave on 1 sq. chocolate, making attractive curls.

Velvet Pie

Baked Crumb Crust, page 11; or baked 9″ pie shell, pages 4–7
1 env. unflavored gelatine
¼ cup cold water
1½ cups milk
3 egg yolks, beaten
¼ cup granulated sugar
⅛ teasp. salt
1 teasp. vanilla extract
3 egg whites
¼ cup granulated sugar
¼ teasp. nutmeg
½ cup heavy cream, whipped
½ sq. unsweetened chocolate

Add gelatine to water; set aside. Scald milk in double boiler; stir slowly into combined yolks, ¼ cup sugar, salt. Cook in double boiler over hot, *not boiling*, water, stirring, until custard coats spoon. Remove; add vanilla, gelatine; stir until melted. Refrigerate, stirring occasionally, until it mounds when dropped from spoon. Beat with beater until *just* smooth. Beat egg whites till they peak when beater is raised; slowly add ¼ cup sugar, beating stiff. Fold into custard. Turn into shell. Sprinkle with nutmeg; refrigerate till set. Top with whipped cream. Shave chocolate on top.

To vary: If preferred, fold whipped cream into custard with egg whites. Refrigerate till it mounds when dropped from spoon, then turn into shell.

Eggnog Pie: Omit vanilla, chocolate; add rum to taste. Use 1 teasp. nutmeg.

Black-Bottom Pie: Make Gingersnap Crust, page 11. Then make above filling, stirring in 2¼ teasp. cornstarch with egg yolks. When added gelatine has melted in custard, stir 1½ sq. melted, unsweetened chocolate and vanilla into half of it. Beat smooth; cool till it mounds; pour into crust; refrigerate. While other half of custard chills till it just begins to set, beat egg whites with sugar, as directed. Fold into chilled custard with 1 tablesp. white rum; pour in as much as shell will hold. Refrigerate a few minutes; pour rest on top. Omit nutmeg; chill till set. Top with whipped cream. Shave ½ sq. chocolate on top.

Candy Velvet Pie (*Pictured on pages 34 and 35*): Omit nutmeg, chocolate and cream if desired. Sprinkle filling with peppermint candy.

Chocolate-Flake Pie: Fold ⅓ cup shaved unsweetened chocolate into filling. Omit chocolate topping.

Nesselrode Pie (*Pictured on page 48*): Substitute 2 tablesp. rum (or rum extract to taste) for vanilla. With whipped cream, fold in ¼ cup diced mixed glacé fruits.

Susan's Christmas Pie: Make Nesselrode Pie, above, in Brazil-Nut Crust, page 11. Substitute ½ cup thinly sliced glacé cherries for mixed glacé fruit.

Coconut Bavarian Pie: Omit nutmeg. With whipped cream, fold in ½ cup flaked coconut. Try, too, with grated fresh coconut, adding ¼ teasp. almond extract with vanilla. Or omit almond; flavor cream with 2 tablesp. crème de menthe. Or top with whipped cream, then generous layer of coconut.

Coffee Velvet Pie (*Pictured on pages 34 and 35*): Make baked 9″ pie shell, pages 4–7, or Nut Crust, page 10. Make filling, adding 2 tablesp. instant coffee to egg whites before beating. Omit cream and shaved chocolate. Melt ¾ cup semi-sweet chocolate pieces over *hot, not boiling* water; stir in ¼ cup water; drizzle on top of the pie. Or fold in ½ cup sliced, pitted dates, ¼ cup chopped pecans with egg whites.

Strawberry Velvet Pie: Fold 1 cup sliced strawberries into filling. Omit chocolate; garnish with strawberries.

Orange Velvet Pie
(*Pictured on page 45*)

1 pkg. piecrust mix
¼ cup orange juice
1 teasp. lemon juice
1 pkg. orange-flavored gelatin
1 cup hot water
1 8-oz. pkg. cream cheese
¼ cup granulated sugar
1 cup heavy cream

1. Prepare 1 baked 9″ pie shell as directed on piecrust-mix package, making high, fluted edge, page 12. While shell bakes, squeeze fruit juices. Dissolve gelatin in hot water.

2. With electric mixer, beat cream cheese until smooth; beat in sugar, orange and lemon juices; then gradually beat in gelatine mixture. Refrigerate until almost set.

3. With electric mixer, whip cream; quickly beat into gelatin mixture; turn into baked pie shell. Refrigerate until set. *Makes 8 servings*

Strawberry-Mallow Cream Pie

Baked 8″ pie shell, pages 4–7
½ lb. large marshmallows
½ cup heavy cream
1 qt. hulled, washed ripe
　strawberries
½ cup heavy cream, whipped

Early in day: In double boiler, melt marshmallows with ½ cup cream. Meanwhile, into baked pie shell, slice or halve strawberries, reserving a few whole ones to decorate top. When marshmallows are melted, set double-boiler top in pan of ice water; with spoon, beat mixture until cold; pour over berries in pie shell. Refrigerate.
To serve: Spread whipped cream over pie and decorate with whole berries.

Cocktail Pie

Baked Gingersnap Crust, page 11
1 No. 2½ can fruit cocktail
1 env. unflavored gelatine
1 tablesp. lemon juice
¼ teasp. salt
1 diced medium banana
1¼ cups heavy cream, whipped
¼ cup confectioners' sugar
¾ teasp. ground ginger
1 tablesp. grated lemon rind

Early in day: Drain fruit cocktail, reserving syrup; soften gelatine in ½ cup of this syrup. Heat another ½ cup syrup; add gelatine; stir until dissolved; stir in lemon juice, salt. Toss drained fruit cocktail with banana; pour in gelatine mixture. Refrigerate until as thick and syrupy as unbeaten egg white. Fold in whipped cream, sugar, ginger, lemon rind. Refrigerate until mixture is stiff enough to hold its shape; turn into baked crust. Refrigerate.

One-Two-Three Strawberry Pie

No-Roll Pastry Shell, page 6
½ cup granulated sugar
1 env. unflavored gelatine
½ cup water
1 10-oz. pkg. frozen sliced
　strawberries
Juice of ½ lemon
⅛ teasp. almond extract
1 cup heavy cream, whipped

1. Prepare and bake pastry shell.
2. While pastry shell cools, make this filling: In saucepan, stir sugar with gelatine. Stir in water; then cook over low heat, stirring, until just below boiling point. Remove from heat. Add unthawed strawberries, lemon juice, almond extract. Stir, breaking up berries with fork, until berries thaw, and mixture thickens. Then fold in whipped cream.
3. Pour filling into baked shell. Refrigerate until set. Pie will be ready to serve in about ½ hr. Garnish with more whipped cream and berries if desired.

Cherry Jubilee Pie

Baked 9″ pie shell, pages 4–7
1 No. 2½ can Bing cherries, pitted
1 pkg. cherry-flavored gelatin
½ cup sherry wine
½ cup heavy cream, whipped
⅓ cup slivered, toasted almonds
½ cup heavy cream, whipped

Early in day: Drain cherries, saving juice. To juice, add enough water to make 1¾ cups liquid; heat. Add gelatin; stir until dissolved. Add sherry; refrigerate until as thick and syrupy as unbeaten egg white. Fold in drained cherries; ½ cup cream, whipped; and almonds. Refrigerate until stiff enough to hold its shape. Turn into baked pie shell. Refrigerate.

To serve: Garnish with remaining ½ cup cream, whipped, plus a few almonds, if desired.

Frosted Daiquiri Pie

Baked 9" pie shell, pages 4–7
1 env. unflavored gelatine
⅔ cup granulated sugar
½ teasp. salt
3 egg yolks
¼ cup cold water
½ cup fresh or canned lime juice
1 teasp. grated lime or lemon rind
Green food color
⅓ cup light rum
3 egg whites
⅓ cup granulated sugar
½ cup heavy cream, whipped

1. In double-boiler top, combine gelatine with ⅔ cup sugar and salt; add egg yolks, water, lime juice; with egg beater, beat until blended. Cook over boiling water (or in saucepan over low heat), stirring, until mixture coats spoon. Remove from heat; add rind; then tint pale green with food color.
2. Cool mixture; stir in rum. Then refrigerate mixture until slightly thicker than unbeaten egg whites. In large bowl, beat egg whites until they form moist peaks when beater is raised; then add ⅓ cup sugar, 1 tablesp. at a time, beating until stiff. Fold in gelatine mixture.
3. Turn mixture into pie shell; refrigerate several hours. Top with whipped cream, sweetened if desired; decorate with short pieces of red cellophane straws.

Grape Chiffon Pie

Baked 9" Graham-Cracker Crust, page 11
1 env. unflavored gelatine
¼ cup cold water
1 6-oz. can frozen grape-juice concentrate
¼ cup granulated sugar
Dash salt
2 tablesp. lemon juice
2 egg whites
½ cup heavy cream, whipped
Allspice

Soften gelatine in cold water. To grape juice, add sugar, salt; bring to boil; stir in gelatine and lemon juice. Refrigerate until partially set. Beat egg whites until stiff; fold in grape mixture. Pour into baked crust. Refrigerate until firm.

To serve: Completely cover top with whipped cream; sprinkle with allspice.

Berry-Patch Parfait Pie

(Pictured on pages 20 and 21)

Baked 9" pie shell, pages 4–7
1 pkg. lemon-flavored gelatin
1¼ cups hot water
1 pt. strawberry ice cream
1½ cups sliced, washed, hulled strawberries
½ cup heavy cream, whipped

About 1 hr. before serving or early in day: In 2-qt. saucepan, dissolve gelatin in hot water. Add ice cream by spoonfuls, stirring until melted. Refrigerate right in pan until thickened but not set— about 15 min. Fold in berries, reserving a few for garnish. Turn into baked pie shell. Refrigerate until set—about 25 min. Garnish with circle of whipped cream. Tuck in reserved strawberry slices.

Fluffy Apricot Pie

Baked 8″ pie shell, pages 4–7
2 cups (½ lb.) dried apricots
1½ cups water
2 teasp. unflavored gelatine
2 tablesp. cold water
3 egg yolks
¼ cup granulated sugar
2 tablesp. fresh, frozen, or canned lemon juice
⅛ teasp. salt
3 egg whites
½ cup granulated sugar
4 drops almond extract
¼ cup heavy cream, whipped

Day before: Soak apricots in water 1 hr.; then cook in same water, covered, 10 min., or until tender. Press apricots and juice through food mill or sieve; then measure 1 cup purée. Soften gelatine in cold water. In double-boiler top, beat egg yolks; stir in ¼ cup sugar, lemon juice, salt, and apricots. Cook over boiling water, stirring, about 5 min., or until mixture just thickens. Add gelatine; stir until dissolved. Refrigerate until as thick and syrupy as unbeaten egg white. Beat egg whites till quite stiff; gradually add ½ cup sugar and extract, beating until stiff. Fold in apricot mixture and whipped cream. Pour into baked pie shell. Refrigerate. **Just before serving:** Garnish with whipped cream.

Cranberry-Fluff Pie

(Pictured on pages 20 and 21)

Baked 9″ pie shell, pages 4–7
1 env. unflavored gelatine
¼ cup cold water
½ cup granulated sugar
⅓ cup cold water
2 egg whites
⅛ teasp. salt
1 tablesp. fresh, frozen, or canned lemon juice
1 teasp. almond extract
1 cup heavy cream
½ large can whole-cranberry sauce
1½ teasp. cornstarch

Early in day: Soften gelatine in ¼ cup cold water. Boil sugar and ⅓ cup water till mixture forms soft ball (235°F. on candy thermometer); stir in gelatine until dissolved. Beat egg whites till quite stiff; slowly pour syrup over them, beating. After all syrup is added, beat 1 min. longer; then add salt, lemon juice, almond extract. Whip cream; fold into gelatine mixture; turn into baked pie shell. Refrigerate until set. In saucepan, combine cranberry sauce, cornstarch; heat till thickened; cool; spread on pie, in star shape. Refrigerate thoroughly before serving. (You may thicken 1 can cranberry sauce with 1 tablesp. cornstarch, and spread over entire pie top as in photo on pages 34 and 35.)

FOUR & TWENTY BLACK BIRDS

Lime-Pineapple Parfait Pie

Baked 9″ pie shell, pages 4–7
Juice drained from No. 2 can
    crushed pineapple, plus water
    to make 1¼ cups
1 pkg. lime-flavored gelatin
1 pt. vanilla ice cream
Drained canned crushed pineapple
    from 1 No. 2 can
Fresh lime slices

1. Bake pie shell; cool.
2. Heat pineapple juice and water in 2-qt. saucepan. Remove from heat; add gelatin, stirring, until gelatin is completely dissolved.
3. Turn ice cream, scoop at a time, into hot gelatin mixture; with blending fork, vigorously stir until ice cream melts and mixes smoothly with gelatin.
4. Chill mixture in refrigerator 25 to 35 min., or until mixture mounds when dropped from spoon. Do not allow it to get too stiff.
5. Spoon 1 cup crushed pineapple onto ice-cream mixture. Fold in; then turn into baked pie shell.
6. Refrigerate pie 25 to 35 min., or till set. To garnish, cut thin slices of lime; with kitchen shears, cut gash in each slice; twist into S shape. Dot top of pie with crushed pineapple and place lime S on each.

Lemon Parfait Pie: Make 8″ Graham-Cracker Crust, page 11, reserving 3 tablesp. crumbs. Use 1 pkg. lemon-flavored gelatin for lime, 1¼ cups water plus 3 tablesp. lemon juice for pineapple juice. Add 1 teasp. grated lemon rind. Omit crushed pineapple and lime slices. Top with reserved crumbs.

Pineapple Parfait Pie: Substitute lemon-flavored gelatin for the lime-flavored gelatin. Garnish with whipped cream. Omit lime slices.

Refrigerator Pineapple Pie

2 tablesp. soft butter or margarine
1½ cups flaked coconut
1 env. unflavored gelatine
¼ cup granulated sugar
3 eggs, separated
1 cup undrained canned crushed pineapple
¼ cup cold water
1 teasp. grated lemon rind
3 tablesp. lemon juice
¼ teasp. salt
6 tablesp. granulated sugar

Early in day: Start heating oven to 350°F. Spread butter evenly on bottom and side of 9″ pie plate. Add coconut, and spread it evenly over butter, pressing down firmly, to form pie shell. Bake 12 to 15 min., or until golden brown; cool.

Meanwhile, mix gelatine and ¼ cup sugar. In double boiler, mix egg yolks with pineapple, water, lemon rind and juice, and gelatine mixture. Cook, stirring frequently, 10 to 15 min., or until smooth and thickened. Remove from heat and cool slightly. Beat egg whites with salt till quite stiff; gradually add 6 tablesp. sugar, beating until stiff. Fold in pineapple mixture. Heap in coconut crust. Refrigerate until serving time. Garnish with whipped cream if desired.

Harvest Chiffon Pie

Baked 9″ pie shell, pages 4–7
1 cup light or dark seedless raisins
1 env. unflavored gelatine
¼ cup milk
3 eggs, separated
1 cup milk
⅓ cup granulated sugar
¾ teasp. cinnamon
1 cup mashed, cooked or canned
    sweet potatoes or yams
⅓ cup granulated sugar

1. Rinse, then drain, raisins. Soften gelatine in ¼ cup milk.
2. In double-boiler top, beat egg yolks well; stir in 1 cup milk, ⅓ cup sugar, cinnamon, sweet potatoes, raisins. Cook over boiling water, stirring, 10 min., or until thickened.
3. Add gelatine; stir until dissolved; refrigerate until as syrupy as unbeaten egg white.
4. Beat egg whites until stiff; slowly add ⅓ cup sugar, beating till stiff.
5. Fold in potato mixture. Heap in pie shell; refrigerate until served.

Pumpkin Chiffon Pie

Baked 9″ pie shell, pages 4–9
1 env. unflavored gelatine
½ cup cold water
2 egg yolks
1 cup undiluted evaporated milk
1¼ cups canned pumpkin
¾ cup dark brown sugar, packed
½ teasp. salt
½ teasp. nutmeg
½ teasp. cinnamon
¼ teasp. ginger
2 egg whites

Day before: Soften gelatine in cold water. In double-boiler top, beat egg yolks; stir in milk, pumpkin, ½ cup brown sugar, salt, nutmeg, cinnamon, ginger. Cook over boiling water, stirring, 10 min. Remove from heat. Add gelatine; stir until dissolved; refrigerate, stirring occasionally, until as thick and syrupy as unbeaten egg white. Beat egg whites until quite stiff; gradually add ¼ cup brown sugar, beating until very stiff. Fold in pumpkin mixture. Turn into baked pie shell. Refrigerate.

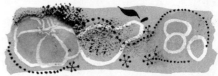

Pear 'n' Cheese Pie

Baked Gingersnap Crust, page 11
1 env. unflavored gelatine
¼ cup cold water
3 egg yolks
2 tablesp. lemon juice
1 teasp. grated lemon rind
¼ cup granulated sugar
½ teasp. salt
1 lb. cottage cheese, sieved
3 egg whites
½ cup granulated sugar
1 cup diced fresh pears (Anjou,
    Bosc, or Comice)

Day before: Soften gelatine in cold water. In double-boiler top, beat egg yolks; stir in lemon juice and rind, ¼ cup sugar, salt. Cook over boiling water, stirring, until mixture thickens; then add softened gelatine; stir until dissolved; remove from heat. Add cottage cheese; refrigerate until as thick and syrupy as unbeaten egg white. Beat egg whites until quite stiff. Gradually add ½ cup sugar, beating until stiff. Fold in gelatine mixture, along with pears. Turn into baked crust. Refrigerate.

Susan's Slipped-Custard Pie

Baked 9″ pie shell, pages 4–7
4 eggs, slightly beaten
½ cup granulated sugar
½ teasp. salt
1 teasp. vanilla extract
2 cups milk
½ teasp. nutmeg

Early in day: Bake shell; cool. Lower heat to 350°F. To eggs, add sugar, salt, vanilla, milk; beat well. "Butter" 9″ pie plate; set in shallow baking pan; strain custard into it; sprinkle with nutmeg. Set in oven; pour hot water into pan to come up three quarters of way on side of plate. Bake 35 min., or till silver knife inserted in center comes out clean. Cool on wire rack.

When shell and custard are cool, tilt custard a bit. With small spatula, gently pull custard away from all sides of plate (*photo A*). To complete loosening, hold plate level with both hands; shake gently. Now hold custard, tilted, over shell, far edge of custard just above, and close to far edge of shell. Shake gently; as custard slips, pull plate back toward you till custard is in shell (*photo B*). Let settle a few minutes.

Serve at once, as is, or top with fruit or berries and whipped cream, toasted coconut, or drizzle of maple-flavored syrup and nuts.

Chocolate-Crested Pie: Melt 1 sq. unsweetened chocolate over very low heat. Stir in 2 tablesp. granulated sugar and 2 tablesp. hot water, a little at a time. Spread over custard after slipping it into shell.

Coconut Custard Pie (*Pictured on pages 34 and 35*): Sprinkle with ½ cup flaked coconut just before or after baking.

Lattice Coconut-Custard Pie: (*Pictured on pages 20 and 21*): Make Coconut Custard Pie, adding coconut to custard just before baking. When pie is completed, melt ⅓ cup semi-sweet chocolate pieces with 1 teasp. vegetable shortening over hot, *not boiling*, water. Dip metal or wooden skewer into this mixture and draw across top of pie in crisscross manner, redipping skewer as needed. Let set; serve.

Wonderful Old-Fashioned Buttermilk Pie

Unbaked 9" pie shell, pages 4–7
2/3 cup granulated sugar
3 tablesp. flour
1/4 teasp. salt
3 egg yolks
2 teasp. vanilla extract
2 cups buttermilk
1/4 cup melted butter or margarine
3 egg whites

Start heating oven to 425°F. With fork, blend sugar, flour, salt; stir in yolks (beaten slightly), vanilla, buttermilk, butter. Beat whites stiff, not dry; slowly beat in yolk mixture. Turn into shell. Bake at 425°F. 10 min., then at 325°F. 30 min., or till knife inserted in center comes out clean. Cool.

Wonderful Walnut Pie

(Pictured on pages 20 and 21)

Unbaked 8" or 9" pie shell,
  pages 4–7
1/2 cup brown sugar, packed
1/2 cup soft butter or margarine
3/4 cup granulated sugar
3 eggs
1/4 teasp. salt
1/4 cup white corn or
  maple-blended syrup
1/2 cup light cream
1 cup broken walnut meats
1/2 teasp. vanilla extract
7 walnut halves

Early in day: Start heating oven to 350°F. Line 8" or 9" pie plate with pastry; make Coin Edge (or Fluted Edge), page 12.

In double-boiler top, cream together brown sugar and butter; stir in granulated sugar, eggs, salt, corn syrup, and cream. Cook over hot, *not boiling*, water 5 min., stirring constantly. Remove from heat; stir in broken nuts and vanilla. Pour into lined pie plate. Bake 50 min. Arrange walnut halves around top. Bake 15 min. longer. Cool on wire rack. (For toasty nuts, bake pie 15 min.; then arrange nuts on top of pie, and bake 50 min.) Nice topped with ice cream.

Peanut Pie: Substitute salted peanuts for broken walnuts. Bake 1 hr. 5 min., omitting extra nuts on top. Serve topped with small mounds of whipped cream and a few peanuts.

Down-South Pecan Pie

(Pictured on pages 34 and 35)

Unbaked 9" pie shell, pages 4–7
1/2 cup butter or margarine
1/2 cup granulated sugar
3/4 cup white corn syrup
1/4 cup maple-flavored syrup, or
  2 tablesp. honey
3 eggs, slightly beaten
1 teasp. vanilla extract
2 cups pecan meats
1 cup heavy cream, whipped

Start heating oven to 350°F. Cream butter well. Add sugar slowly, creaming till light. Slowly stir in syrups, eggs, vanilla, 1 cup nuts. Pour into shell. Top with rest of nuts. Bake 55 min. Cool. Serve small wedges with whipped cream, flavored with sherry if desired. Nice with small bunches of grapes.

Fudge-Nut Pie *(Pictured on pages 34 and 35)*: Reduce butter to 1/4 cup, pecans (or almonds) to 1 cup. Add 2 sq. melted unsweetened chocolate to butter.

Coconut Pie: Substitute 1 1/2 cups flaked coconut for pecans, lemon juice for vanilla; add 1/2 teasp. salt.

Pilgrim Pumpkin or Squash Pie

Unbaked 9″ pie shell, pages 4–7
1¾ cups canned pumpkin or
  thawed frozen squash
¾ cup brown sugar, firmly packed
¾ teasp. salt
1 teasp. cinnamon
½ teasp. ginger
½ teasp. nutmeg
1 cup undiluted evaporated milk
½ cup water
2 eggs, well beaten

PILGRIM PUMPKIN PIE

Refrigerate pie shell several hours. Heat pumpkin (or thawed squash) over low heat 10 min., stirring often, to dry out slightly. Start heating oven to 450°F. Combine sugar, salt, cinnamon, ginger, and nutmeg. Stir into pumpkin. Stir milk, water, pumpkin mixture, into eggs. Strain through fine strainer. Pour most of it into shell. Place on oven rack; add rest of filling. Bake at 450°F. 15 min.; reduce heat to 300°F.; bake 45 min., or until silver knife inserted in center comes out clean. Cool on rack. *P.S.*—1 tablesp. brandy may be added.
To serve: Top each wedge with whipped cream and honey; vanilla or coffee ice cream; or packaged cheese slices cut in shape of pumpkin, turkey, or leaf. Or serve as is with cheese wedges.
Nut-Pumpkin Pie: Sprinkle ½ cup sliced Brazil nuts, almonds, filberts, peanuts, pecans, or walnuts on pie 10 min. before it's done.

IN THE COLOR PHOTO ON PAGE 45—*Top row, left to right:* Spiced Peach Crunch Pie, page 18; Orange Velvet Pie, page 37; Double Cream Pie, page 29. *Middle row:* Hearts Delight Tarts, page 58. *In front:* Envelope Pie, page 23; Lunch-Box Pineapple Crusties, page 61.

Susan's Walnut-Fudge Pie

Unbaked 9″ pie shell, pages 4–7
2 sq. unsweetened chocolate
½ cup light-brown sugar, packed
¼ cup soft butter or margarine
¾ cup granulated sugar
3 eggs, unbeaten
¼ teasp. salt
½ cup milk or light cream
¼ cup corn syrup
1 cup finely chopped walnuts
1 teasp. vanilla extract
¼ cup broken walnut meats

1. Start heating oven to 350°F.
2. In double boiler, melt chocolate; remove from water. Add brown sugar, butter; beat until well blended.
3. Add granulated sugar; mix well. Add eggs, one at a time, beating after each addition till blended. Add salt, milk, corn syrup; mix well.
4. Cook over boiling water, stirring, 5 min. Remove from water; stir in 1 cup finely chopped walnuts and vanilla. Pour into unbaked pie shell.
5. Bake 1 hr.; scatter ¼ cup broken walnuts on top; bake 5 min. Serve warm. Or make day before; refrigerate; then to serve, warm at 350°F. 15 min.

Pineapple-Cheese Pie

(Pictured on pages 34 and 35)

Unbaked 9″ pie shell, pages 4–7
1 cup well-drained, canned
crushed pineapple
¾ cup granulated sugar
4 3-oz. pkgs. softened cream cheese
1 tablesp. flour
4 eggs, slightly beaten
¼ cup light cream or undiluted
evaporated milk
¼ cup milk
1 teasp. vanilla extract

Bake pie shell at 450°F. 10 min.; cool; cover bottom with pineapple. Blend sugar, cream cheese, and flour. To eggs, add cream, milk, and vanilla; blend with cheese mixture. Pour into shell. Bake at 350°F. 45 min., or till firm to the touch (will be pale). Serve as is, or top with slivered almonds or walnuts, sautéed in butter. Or spread with jam.

Max's Super Cheese Pie

Unbaked Graham-Cracker Crust,
page 10
4 3-oz. pkgs. softened cream cheese
2 eggs
½ cup granulated sugar
½ teasp. vanilla extract
1 cup commercial sour cream

Start heating oven to 350°F. Beat cheese, eggs, sugar, vanilla, with hand or electric beater until creamy. Turn into shell. Bake 35 min. Spread sour cream on top; cool. Serve as is, or topped with sliced strawberries or peaches.

Jubilee Cheese Pie: Start heating oven to 425°F. Use unbaked 9″ pie shell, pages 4–7; into it turn 1 No. 2 can cherry pie-filling mix. Bake 15 min.,

then reduce oven temperature to 350°F. Meanwhile, mix cheese, eggs, sugar, vanilla as above; spoon over cherry filling. Bake 30 min. Cool; top with sour cream; sprinkle with nutmeg.

Ellen's Chocolate Cheese Pie: Make as above, except: Increase sugar to ⅔ cup. Into cheese mixture, fold 2 sq. unsweetened chocolate, melted, cooled. Omit sour cream.

Whipped-Cheese Pie

Unbaked 9″ pie shell, pages 4–7
1½ cups cottage cheese
3 egg yolks
¾ cup granulated sugar
3 tablesp. all-purpose flour
¼ teasp. salt
¾ cup undiluted evaporated milk
¾ teasp. vanilla extract
3 egg whites
Nutmeg

Early in day: Start heating oven to 400°F. In large mixer bowl, with electric mixer at medium speed, or "cream,"* beat cheese until fairly smooth; add egg yolks; beat well. Stir in sugar mixed with flour and salt; beat till smooth. Beat in evaporated milk and vanilla. Beat egg whites till stiff; fold into cheese mixture. Pour into unbaked pie shell; sprinkle lightly with nutmeg. Bake at 400°F. 10 min.; reduce oven temperature to 350°F.; bake 30 min. longer, or until firm. Cool on wire rack; refrigerate.
*If mixing by hand, press cheese through wire strainer; then add egg yolks, and make as directed, beating with spoon.

Take Pie Shells

Recipes: Prepare pastry for one-crust pies, pages 4 to 7.

Freezing: *Unbaked*—Leave shells in pie plates. For easier handling, first freeze unwrapped; then wrap at once in moisture-vaporproof material. They can be stacked in freezer if padding of crumpled waxed paper is put between each of the wrapped shells. *Baked*—Cool shells at room temperature; then freeze and wrap, in or out of plates as desired. They can be stacked in freezer. Since pie shells are fragile, tuck in a safe place in freezer; store a few at one time.

Thawing: *Unbaked*—Unwrap frozen shell; bake at 450°F. 5 min.; reprick; bake about 15 min. Or let stand, wrapped, at room temperature 30 min.; then unwrap and bake 12 min., repricking after first 5 min. *Baked*—Unwrap frozen shell; heat at 375°F. about 10 min., or until thawed. Or thaw, wrapped, at room temperature.

IN THE COLOR PHOTO ON PAGE 48 —Nesselrode Pie, page 37. **ON PAGE 49**—Ellen's Sundae Pie, page 64.

Take Cream or Custard Pies

These pies do not freeze well. However, baked pumpkin pie may be frozen for short storage; for longer storage, freeze unbaked filling, ready to pour into pie shell, or freeze filling in shell before wrapping. Thaw before baking.

Take Two-Crust or Deep-Dish Pies

Recipes: Apple, peach, cherry,* blueberry, mince, strawberry rhubarb, pages 13 to 26. Use 2 to 4 tablesp. flour, depending on the juiciness of the fruit.

Freezing: *Unbaked*—Do not make slits in top crust. Wrap as in Take Chiffon Pies, page 51. Use within 2 months, while at their highest quality. *Baked*—Cool baked pies thoroughly at room temperature; then wrap. Place level in freezer to prevent juices from dripping. Use within 3 months.

Thawing: *Unbaked*—Remove wrappings from frozen pie; make slits in top crust. Bake at 425°F., 40 to 60 min., for deep-dish pie, 45 to 60 min. for two-crust pie. *Baked*—Remove wrappings from frozen pie. Heat at 375°F., 30 to 50 min. for deep-dish pie, 35 to 50 min. for two-crust pie.

*Freeze fresh cherry pie after baking.

Take Chiffon Pies

Recipes: Lemon, orange, chocolate, Nesselrode, pages 32 to 37. Make them in regular pie plates. Or use foil or paper ones with metal rims both for baking and freezing.

Freezing: After pies are set, cover with a second pie plate, preferably a foil or paper one. (This allows you to stack the pies in the freezer, and protects them, too.) Next, wrap covered pie with moisture-vaporproof film, foil, or freezer paper; seal. Label, date, and freeze. Plan to use them within at least 3 months.

Thawing: Unwrap frozen pie and let it stand in food compartment of refrigerator 1 to 2 hrs. Top with whipped cream while still frozen or just before serving.

Freezer Lemon Meringue Pie

Baked 8″ pie shell, pages 4–7
1 cup granulated sugar
¼ cup cornstarch
⅛ teasp. salt
1¼ cups warm water
Grated rind of 1 lemon
¼ cup lemon juice
3 egg yolks, slightly beaten
1 tablesp. butter or margarine
2 egg whites
¼ teasp. salt
¼ cup granulated sugar

On any cool day: In double boiler combine 1 cup sugar, cornstarch, ⅛ teasp. salt. Slowly stir in water, then lemon rind and juice, egg yolks, butter. Cook over boiling water, stirring constantly, until mixture is thick enough to mound when dropped from spoon. Cool; then spoon into cooled pie shell. Freezer-wrap, first covering pie with second pie plate (preferably a paper one). Freeze; plan to use within a month or so, adding meringue (below) just before serving.

About 1 hr. before serving: Start heating oven to 350°F. Beat egg whites with ¼ teasp. salt until frothy; gradually add ¼ cup sugar, beating until stiff peaks are formed. *Now* take pie from freezer; unwrap. Spoon meringue over pie, being sure to spread it out to crust edge all around. Bake 20 min., or till meringue is tinged with brown. Cool on wire rack about 1 hr. When you cut pie, meringue will be deliciously runny and marshmallowlike.

Peach Ice-Cream Pie

1 cup granulated sugar
¼ teasp. cream of tartar
4 egg whites
2 qts. vanilla ice cream
Frozen or fresh sliced peaches (or strawberries or raspberries)

Start heating oven to 275°F. To make meringue, sift sugar with cream of tartar; beat egg whites until stiff; gradually add sifted sugar and continue beating until glossy. "Butter" 2 9″ pie plates; spread meringue on bottoms and sides of pie plates, swirling it up at edges and keeping it off rims of plates. Bake 1 hr. Cool; wrap carefully; freeze.

To serve: Unwrap; thaw meringue shells at room temperature 15 min. Fill with rounded spoonfuls of ice cream. Cover with peaches, barely thawed. If desired, top with whipped cream and almonds.

Makes 2 pies, 16 servings

Frozen Sherry-Almond Pie

2 cups finely ground almonds
3 tablesp. granulated sugar
1 env. unflavored gelatine
¼ cup cold water
1½ cups milk
2 egg yolks, unbeaten
⅛ teasp. salt
⅓ cup granulated sugar
2 egg whites
⅓ cup granulated sugar
1 cup heavy cream, whipped
2 tablesp. sherry (or 1½ teasp.
   vanilla extract and ½ teasp.
   almond extract)
1 cup heavy cream*

Several weeks in advance: Start heating oven to 400°F. Combine 1½ cups ground almonds with 3 tablesp. sugar; use to cover bottom and side of 9″ pie plate, pressing against side of plate with back of spoon. Bake 8 min.; cool. Meanwhile, soften gelatine in cold water. Scald milk in double boiler. Combine egg yolks, salt, ⅓ cup sugar; add milk slowly, stirring constantly. Return mixture to double boiler. Cook over hot, *not boiling*, water, stirring constantly, until thick enough to coat spoon with thin film of custard—about 5 min. Remove from heat; stir in gelatine; cool. Refrigerate until quite thick but not lumpy. Beat egg whites until stiff; beat in ⅓ cup sugar. Into custard, fold egg

whites; 1 cup cream, whipped; sherry; and reserved ½ cup nuts. Pour into pie shell. Refrigerate until set. Then pour on any leftover mixture; refrigerate until set. Wrap for freezing; freeze.

Early in day: Unwrap pie; thaw in food compartment of refrigerator about 2 hrs. At serving time, spread whipped cream over top.   *Makes 8 servings*

*For cream topping, you may substitute 1 6-oz. pkg. semisweet-chocolate pieces melted with 1 tablesp. vegetable shortening over hot, *not boiling*, water.

P.S.—If preferred, make pie early in day; then refrigerate.

Orange-Lime Chiffon Pie

2 Baked 9″ pie shells, pages 4–7
1 tablesp. unflavored gelatine
⅔ cup orange juice
8 eggs, separated
⅔ cup granulated sugar
2 tablesp. grated orange rind
½ cup lime (or lemon) juice
½ teasp. salt
1 cup granulated sugar
1 cup heavy cream, whipped

Make and bake pie shells; cool. Sprinkle gelatine on orange juice; set aside. Place egg yolks in double-boiler top; add ⅔ cup sugar, orange rind, and lime juice; stir until smooth. Cook over boiling water, stirring constantly, 5 min., or until thickened. Add gelatine; stir well; remove from heat. Beat egg whites with salt until stiff; gradually beat in 1 cup sugar; fold into hot orange mixture. Pour into pie shells. Refrigerate until set; carefully wrap and freeze.

To serve: Unwrap; thaw in food compartment of refrigerator about 2 hrs. Top with whipped cream.

Makes 2 pies, 12 to 16 servings

IN THE COLOR PHOTO ON PAGE 52—
Baked-Alaska Pie, page 64.

Frozen Coffee Pie

1½ cups ground Brazil nuts, walnuts, or pecans (use medium
 blade)
¼ cup granulated sugar
⅛ teasp. salt
1 egg white
1 tablesp. instant coffee
½ cup milk
16 marshmallows
1 egg yolk
1 cup heavy cream, whipped
¼ teasp. almond extract

Several days ahead or early in day: Start
heating oven to 375°F. "Butter" 9″ pie
plate; line bottom with circle of waxed
paper; butter. Mix nuts, sugar, salt.
Beat egg white until it forms soft peaks;
add to nut mixture; mix well. Press
firmly to bottom and side (not rim) of
pie plate. Bake 12 to 15 min., or till
light brown. With small spatula, carefully loosen around sides; let stand 10
min. Lift crust; slip out paper; let cool.
Meanwhile, in saucepan, combine coffee,
milk, marshmallows; cook over low
heat, stirring, till marshmallows melt.
Beat egg yolk lightly; stir in small
amount of hot mixture; return to saucepan. Cook 1 min. longer, stirring. Refrigerate, stirring occasionally, until
thickened but not set. Fold in cream,
extract; turn into cooled crust. Place
in freezer until served. (If storing several days, freezer-wrap when firm.)
To serve: Garnish with whipped cream,
and sprinkle with instant coffee.
Note: Can be made early on day of serving and refrigerated until well chilled.

Harlequin Pies

3 cups crushed chocolate wafers
6 tablesp. soft butter or margarine
2 env. unflavored gelatine
½ cup cold water
3 cups milk
6 egg yolks, beaten
½ cup granulated sugar
¼ teasp. salt
4 teasp. cornstarch
2 teasp. vanilla extract
3 sq. unsweetened chocolate
6 egg whites
½ cup granulated sugar
2 tablesp. white rum
1 cup heavy cream
Unsweetened chocolate, shaved

Using fork, mix wafer crumbs with butter until crumbly. With back of spoon,
press to bottoms and sides of 2 9″ pie
plates. Bake at 375°F. 8 min.; cool. Add
gelatine to water; set aside. Scald milk
in double boiler; slowly stir into egg
yolks, ½ cup sugar, salt, and cornstarch,
combined. Cook, stirring, over hot, *not
boiling* water, until custard coats spoon.
Remove from heat; add gelatine; stir
until melted. To half of custard, add
vanilla, 3 sq. melted chocolate; beat
until smooth. Refrigerate until mixture
mounds; pour into 2 crusts; refrigerate.

Refrigerate other half of custard till
it just begins to set. Meanwhile, beat
egg whites till they form peaks when
beater is raised. Slowly add ½ cup
sugar, beating till stiff. Fold egg whites
and rum into custard. Spoon over chocolate mixture in shells; refrigerate until
set; wrap; freeze.
To serve: Thaw pies, unwrapped, in food
compartment of refrigerator 2 hrs. Just
before serving, top with whipped cream
and shaved chocolate.

Makes 2 pies, 16 servings

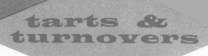

Baked Tart Shells

Prepare Packaged Piecrust Mix, page 7, or any pastry, pages 4 to 7. Make tart shells as shown in photos on pages 56 and 57. After pricking well, refrigerate ½ hr.; bake (on baking sheet if desired) at 450°F. 10 to 15 min., or until golden brown. Cool on wire rack. Carefully lift from pans or sheet.

For unbaked tart shells: Prepare pastry as above, or as recipe directs. Fill and bake as in individual recipes.

Fillings: Any fresh, frozen or canned fruit; any drained, stewed, fresh or canned fruit; any cream, custard or chiffon filling (see pie recipes); apple-sauce, apple butter, etc.

Toppings: Toasted or plain, flaked coconut; sweetened whipped cream (add grated orange rind, vanilla or almond extract, sherry or brandy, or coconut); vanilla ice cream, with chopped nuts, cinnamon, or flaked chocolate; whipped sour cream or cream cheese, or cottage cheese; meringue topping (see page 67); blobs of cheese spread; or cheese-roll slices; chocolate or butterscotch sauce, or any sundae topping, if ice-cream-filled tarts.

Glazes: Heat ¼ to ½ cup currant or apple jelly with 1 tablesp. water till it melts. Use over berries, peaches, pineapple, etc. Or blend 1 tablesp. cornstarch with 1 tablesp. water. Stir into ⅔ cup juice from cooked or canned fruit. Boil clear. Add 1 teasp. lemon juice.   *Enough glaze for 8 to 10 tarts*

Baked Open Tarts
(Pictured on pages 34 and 35)

Line muffin or tart pans with pastry having fluted edge, page 12, or as in Petal Tarts, page 56. Fill as in Pilgrim Pumpkin Pie, page 46, Down-South Pecan Pie, page 44, or Mince Pie, page 23, reducing baking time as needed—usually 10 to 20 min. Garnish as in large-pie recipe.

Pielets
(Pictured on pages 34 and 35)

Little two-crust pies, just right for small families, can be made in individual glass or metal pie plates, or in muffin pans. Fit pastry in plates or muffin pans; fill, cover, and bake as in apple, berry or fruit, cherry, rhubarb, mince, or raisin pies, pages 14 to 23. Allow about 5 to 10 min. less baking time, or until done. Serve as in large pies.

Note: Some of today's frozen "pielets" are nice, too.

55

Petal Tart Shells: Cut 6 2¼″ pastry rounds; lay one in bottom of custard cup or 2¾″ muffin-pan cup. Wet edges; press 5 rounds to sides and bottom of cup, overlapping.

Fluted Tart Shells: Measure fluted tart pans; cut pastry rounds as for Pleated Tart Shells, page 57. Fit rounds over inverted pans, using side of wooden skewer to mark grooves.

Floweret Tart Shells: Cut 5″ pastry squares with knife or pastry wheel. Snugly fit one square inside of each 2¾″ muffin-pan cup, allowing corners to stand upright.

Shortcake Tart Shells: Cut out pastry rounds with 3½″ biscuit cutter. Remove centers from half rounds with 1½″ cutter. Arrange on ungreased baking sheet.

Lemon Cream-Cheese Tarts

6 baked 3¾″ (across top) Fluted
   Tart Shells, pages 56 and 57
3 eggs
⅔ cup granulated sugar
⅓ cup lemon juice
2 teasp. grated lemon rind
3 3-oz. pkg. softened cream cheese
6 teasp. grape jelly

Beat eggs until thick and fluffy, in top of double boiler; continue beating while gradually adding sugar, lemon juice, lemon rind. Cook over boiling water, stirring constantly, till thick; gradually stir into cheese. Cool; fill shells. Top with bit of jelly. *Makes 6 tarts*

Cherry Tarts

8 baked Floweret Tart Shells,
   pages 56 and 57
1 No. 2 can pitted red sour cherries
   (water packed)
¾ cup granulated sugar
2 tablesp. cornstarch
¼ teasp. salt
¾ cup cherry juice
1 teasp. grated lemon rind
¼ teasp. almond extract

Drain cherries. Combine sugar, cornstarch, salt in saucepan; stir in juice. Boil, stirring, till thick and clear. Add rind, extract, cherries. Cool; fill shells. Top with ice cream. *Makes 8 tarts*

Jellied Cherry Tarts

8 baked Petal Tart Shells,
   pages 55 and 56
1 pkg. cherry-flavored gelatin
1½ cups juice drained from
   cherries plus water
2 cups pitted canned Bing cherries
4 to 6 tablesp. sherry
½ cup heavy cream, whipped; or
   1 3-oz. pkg. cream cheese

Dissolve gelatin in hot cherry juice.
Add cherries and sherry. Refrigerate
till set. Run spatula around each tart
shell; remove from pan.

At serving time: Break up gelatin with
fork; spoon into tart shells. (Spoon any
leftover gelatin into sherbet glasses.)
Place whipped cream on top (or use
cream cheese mixed with 2 tablesp. milk
until smooth). Sprinkle with almonds,
if desired.   *Makes 8 servings*

For two-in-one party: Make twice recipe.
Leave half of tart shells in pan; for
second party, reheat in 425°F. oven 3
min. Let gelatin stand at room temperature 15 min. before serving.

Orange Tea Tartlets

1 pkg. piecrust mix
2 teasp. grated orange rind
3 to 4 tablesp. orange juice
Jelly, preserves or marmalade
Chopped nuts

Start heating oven to 450°F. Blend rind
with piecrust mix; add orange juice;
mix lightly with fork. Shape into ball.
Roll half of dough at a time, ⅛″ thick.
Cut with 3″ scalloped cookie cutter. Fit
rounds in muffin-pan cups (about 2″
across top); prick with fork. Bake 10 to
12 min. Fill with jelly, top with nuts.

Makes 22 tartlets

Pleated Tart Shells: Invert muffin pan. With a
piece of cord, measure one of muffin-pan
cups—up one side, across bottom, and down
other side. Cut cord to this length. Cut out
pastry rounds with pastry wheel, using saucer,
small pie plate, or floured cardboard pattern
having diameter equal to length of string.

Fit pastry round over outside of one cup of
inverted muffin pan, pinching it into 6 or 7
pleats to fit snugly. Repeat on alternate
muffin-pan cups so tarts will brown evenly.
With a 4-tined fork, prick tarts evenly across
bottom. Refrigerate ½ hr. Prick again. Bake
at 450°F. 10 to 15 min. Fill and top as desired.

Luscious Cream Tarts

Prepare pastry for tart shells, pages 4–7. Bake as recipe below directs.

Satin-Smooth Cream Tarts (*Pictured on pages 34 and 35*): Partly fill baked Fluted Tart Shells, pages 55 and 56, with Satin-Smooth Cream Pie filling, page 28. Top with whole green grapes and orange sections folded into fruit-gelatin dessert. Refrigerate.

Butterscotch-Banana Cream Tarts (*Pictured on pages 34 and 35*): Fill baked Fluted Tart Shells, pages 55 and 56, with Butterscotch Cream Pie filling, page 28. Top with banana slices and whipped cream.

Lemon-Cream Shortcake Tarts (*Pictured on pages 34 and 35*): Bake Shortcake Tart Shells, pages 55 and 56, saving centers cut from half of rounds with biscuit cutter. Fill with Lemon Meringue Pie filling, page 27; top with whipped cream.

Sherried Prune Tarts

6 or 8 baked Floweret Tart Shells,
    pages 55 and 56
2 cups large dried prunes
3 lemon slices
¾ cup prune liquid
¾ cup sherry
1 tablesp. cornstarch
1 tablesp. water
½ cup heavy cream

Cook prunes with lemon, as label directs; drain. Boil down prune liquid to ¾ cup; add sherry; pour over prunes in shallow dish; refrigerate 4 hrs. Drain off liquid; stir in cornstarch mixed with water. Boil until thick and clear. Add pitted prunes; refrigerate; fill shells; top with whipped cream. *Makes 6 or 8 tarts*

Heart's Delight Tarts

(*Pictured on page 45*)

1 pkg. piecrust mix
1 qt. strawberries
1 tablesp. cornstarch
¼ cup water
⅓ cup white corn syrup
Vanilla ice cream

1. Start heating oven to 475°F. From foil, cut out 16 heart shapes, 4½″ long by 4½″ wide at widest point. Prepare piecrust mix as label directs; on lightly floured surface, roll it out ⅛″ thick. Using foil heart as pattern, cut out 8 hearts. Place pastry heart between 2 foil hearts; turn up edges ½″ all around, pinching together as necessary to form heart-shaped shell. Set on baking sheet. Bake 6 to 8 min., or until golden; cool a few minutes; peel off foil.

2. *About 1 hr. before serving:* Hull the strawberries; with fork, crush just enough to make ¼ cup crushed strawberries. For glaze, in small saucepan, mix crushed berries, cornstarch, and water; then stir in corn syrup. Cook, stirring, until thickened, clear.

3. Into 4 heart shells drop rest of strawberries; with spoon, drizzle glaze over berries. Refrigerate.

4. At serving time, place several spoonfuls of ice cream in remaining heart shells. Serve 1 strawberry-filled and 1 ice-cream-filled heart to each person. *Makes 8 servings*

Pecan Tarts

8 or 9 unbaked Petal Tart Shells,
pages 55 and 56
¼ cup soft butter or margarine
¼ cup granulated sugar
⅓ cup light corn syrup
2 tablesp. maple syrup or dark corn
syrup
2 eggs, slightly beaten
½ teasp. vanilla extract
Dash salt
1 cup whole pecan meats
½ cup heavy cream, whipped

Start heating oven to 325°F. With back
of spoon, cream butter against sides of
medium bowl until creamy. Gradually
add sugar, continuing to work until
smooth and creamy. Slowly stir in corn
and maple syrups. Then add eggs,
vanilla, and salt; stir to blend. Spoon
into chilled, unbaked tart shells. Sprinkle
nuts on top; push nuts down so filling
covers them slightly. Bake 45 min., or
until pastry is golden and knife inserted
into center of filling comes out clean.

Let tarts cool in pan. Then run
spatula between pastry and cups; place
wire rack over muffin pan; turn out,
right side up.

To serve: Top each tart with dab of
whipped cream. Place tiny bunch of
seedless grapes on each plate, as a fin-
ishing and decorative touch.

Makes 8 or 9 tarts

Swedish Toscas

6 tablesp. butter or margarine
¼ cup granulated sugar
1 cup sifted all-purpose flour
⅓ cup slivered blanched almonds
¼ cup granulated sugar
2 tablesp. butter or margarine
1½ tablesp. light or heavy cream
2 teasp. flour

1. Start heating oven to 350°F.
2. Mix 6 tablesp. butter with ¼ cup
   sugar until very light and fluffy.
   Blend in 1 cup flour.
3. Divide mixture into 12 parts; press
   one part into bottom and halfway up
   sides of each of 12 ungreased 2¼″
   muffin-pan cups. Bake 10 min.
4. Meanwhile, in saucepan, combine
   almonds, ¼ cup sugar, 2 tablesp.
   butter, cream, 2 teasp. flour. Heat
   over low heat, stirring constantly,
   until mixture boils; remove.
5. Spoon mixture into partially baked
   cookie shells. Bake 15 min., or until
   brown. Cool in muffin-pan cups 3 to 5
   min.; then carefully remove.

Makes 1 doz.

Party Tarts

3 cups crisp rice cereal
¼ lb. large marshmallows
2 tablesp. butter or margarine
Vanilla ice cream

Put cereal in greased large bowl. Cook
marshmallows with butter over hot
water until syrupy; then pour over
cereal, stirring briskly. With buttered
hands, quickly press enough of mixture
into each 3¾″ (across top) fluted tart
pan to line bottom, side. Let set at least
1 hr.; lift out. Fill with ice cream. Top
with berries or chocolate sauce.

Makes 6 to 8 tarts

Mince Turnovers

1. Make pastry, pages 4–7. Roll out half into rectangle ⅛″ thick. (Use other half to make Applesauce Turnovers, on this page.) With pastry wheel or small paring knife, cut into 5 or 6 4″ squares (*photo A*).
2. Place 1 tablesp. mincemeat in corner of each square (*photo B*). Moisten edges with water, using fingers. Fold from one corner to opposite.
3. Firmly seal edges of each with floured fork (*photo C*). Split or prick top with skewer. Glaze, page 66. Bake as in Applesauce Turnovers.

Makes 5 to 6 turnovers

Applesauce Turnovers

1. Roll other half of pastry for Mince Turnovers ⅛″ thick; cut into 4½″ rounds (*photo D*). Place a tablesp. applesauce on each half round; wet edges with water.
2. Fold so edges come together; press. Seal edges (use blunt end of wooden skewer, or flute with fingers). Slit or prick top with skewer (*photo E*). Glaze, page 66.
3. Place on ungreased baking sheet with Mince Turnovers. Bake at 450°F. about 15 min. Serve warm with cheese cubes.   *Makes 5 to 6 turnovers*

Almond Turnovers

Mix 1 beaten egg, ½ cup sugar, 2 tablesp. soft butter, 1 cup ground blanched almonds, 1 teasp. almond extract. Roll 2 pkg. piecrust mix ⅛″ thick; cut 34 3¼″ scalloped rounds. Drop ½ teasp. raspberry jam on each, 1 teasp. almond mixture on top of jam. Seal; slit; bake as Applesauce Turnovers, page 60.

Makes 34 turnovers

Cream-Cheese Turnovers
(Pictured on pages 34 and 35)

Delicious as dessert or for tea. Especially easy to make in cold weather.

With pastry blender, blend 3 3-oz. pkgs. cream cheese with ½ cup butter. Blend in 1½ cups sifted all-purpose flour; refrigerate overnight. Start heating oven to 450°F. Roll pastry ⅛″ thick; cut, seal as in Mince Turnovers, page 60, using any of fillings below. Prick; glaze, page 66. Bake 15 min., or until golden. Dust with confectioners' sugar.

Fillings: Use canned whole- or jellied-cranberry sauce; orange marmalade, chopped nuts; apple butter or applesauce; chopped nuts; strawberry jam.

Lunch-Box Pineapple Crusties
(Pictured on page 45)

½ cup brown sugar, packed
½ teasp. cinnamon
3 tablesp. soft butter or margarine
1 No. 2 can pineapple chunks
1 pkg. piecrust mix

1. Start heating oven to 425°F. With fork, mix sugar with cinnamon, butter. Drain pineapple chunks well.
2. Make piecrust as label directs. Roll into 18″x12″ rectangle; cut into 3″ squares. Lay 1 pineapple chunk in center of each square; sprinkle with sugar mixture.
3. Bring four corners of each square to center; then press all edges together well. Brush with cream, if desired. Place on baking sheet; bake 10 min., or until golden. *Makes 24 crusties*

Banbury Turnovers

¼ cup chopped walnuts
½ cup seedless raisins
¼ cup snipped figs
½ cup brown sugar, firmly packed
1 tablesp. flour
2 tablesp. lemon juice
1 tablesp. grated lemon rind
Pastry, pages 4–7; or Cheese Pastry, page 4

Start heating oven to 450°F. Mix walnuts, raisins, figs, sugar, flour, lemon juice, and lemon rind. Roll pastry ⅛″ thick; cut into 4″ squares. Place 1 tablesp. filling in corner of each. Moisten edges with water; fold from one corner to within ¼″ of opposite. Turn lower edge up over top; press; flute, page 12; glaze, page 66. Slit. Bake 15 min., or till golden. *Makes 12 turnovers*

Strawberry Angel Pie

½ cup granulated sugar
⅛ teasp. cream of tartar
2 egg whites
⅓ cup chopped almonds
1 pt. strawberries, halved
Whipped cream (optional)

Start heating oven to 275°F. Sift sugar and cream of tartar together. With egg beater or electric mixer, beat egg whites until stiff but not dry. Add sifted ingredients slowly, beating continuously until smooth and glossy. Use mixture to line bottom and side of well-greased 9″ pie plate, keeping center hollowed out to ¼″ thickness (do not spread meringue on rim). Sprinkle with nuts. Bake about 1 hr., or until lightly browned and crisp to touch. Cool.

Just before serving: Fill with sliced, sweetened strawberries and top with whipped cream.

To vary: Replace berries with orange sections or cut-up pineapple.

Mocha Angel Pie

(Pictured on pages 20 and 21)

3 egg whites
¼ teasp. cream of tartar
Dash salt
¾ cup granulated sugar
2 6-oz. pkgs. (2 cups) semisweet-chocolate pieces
1 tablesp. instant coffee
¼ cup boiling water
1 cup heavy cream, whipped
1 teasp. vanilla extract

Early in day or day before: Start heating oven to 275°F. Beat egg whites until quite stiff; gradually add cream of tartar, salt, and sugar, beating until stiff and satiny. Spread about two thirds of this meringue over bottom and side of well-greased 8″ pie plate. Drop remaining meringue, in mounds, along rim of plate, pulling each mound up into points. Bake 1 hr., or until shell is light brown and crisp. Cool on wire rack, away from drafts.

In double-boiler top over hot, *not boiling*, water, melt chocolate pieces. Combine instant coffee and boiling water; stir into melted chocolate. Cool 5 min., stirring now and then; fold into whipped cream with vanilla. Pour into meringue shell. Refrigerate.

Strawberry-Marshmallow Pie

"Baked" in the refrigerator.

24 large marshmallows
¼ cup warm water
10 graham crackers, rolled into crumbs
1 cup heavy cream, whipped
3 cups halved strawberries, or whole raspberries or blueberries
1 cup whole berries, for garnish

In saucepan, melt marshmallows in warm water; chill till *completely* cool but *not* set. Grease 9″ pie plate with butter or margarine; sprinkle with all except 2 tablesp. graham-cracker crumbs. Stir up marshmallows; fold in cream, then 3 cups berries. Spoon lightly into shell, piling high in center; arrange 1 cup berries on top; sprinkle reserved crumbs around edge. Refrigerate.

Chocolate-Mousse Pie

(*Pictured on pages 34 and 35*)

Baked 9″ pie shell, pages 4–7; or
   Chocolate Crumb Crust, page 11
1 6-oz. pkg. semisweet-chocolate
   pieces
1 egg
2 egg yolks
1 teasp. rum
2 egg whites
1¼ cups heavy cream
½ sq. unsweetened chocolate

Melt semisweet-chocolate pieces over hot water; remove; beat in egg, yolks, one at a time; add rum. Beat whites till they peak when beater is raised; whip 1 cup cream; fold both into chocolate mixture. Spoon into shell. Refrigerate. Top with ¼ cup cream, whipped; shave on unsweetened chocolate.
Angel Pie: Make Meringue Crust, page 31. Fill with Chocolate Mousse, above, (halve each ingredient except the 1 egg); refrigerate 12 to 24 hrs.

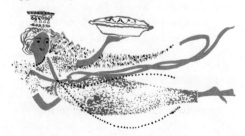

Fudge Pie Alamode

3 sq. unsweetened chocolate
⅓ cup butter or margarine
2 cups granulated sugar
4 eggs
⅔ cup chopped walnuts
¼ teasp. salt
1 teasp. vanilla extract
1 pt. vanilla ice cream

Day before: Start heating oven to 350°F. In double boiler, melt chocolate and butter, stirring. Cool slightly. Stir in sugar. In large bowl, beat eggs; stir in chocolate mixture, then nuts, salt, and vanilla. Pour into well-greased 9″ pie plate. Bake 45 to 50 min. Cool on wire rack. Refrigerate.
Just before serving: Cut pie into wedges; serve topped with ice cream.

Coffee Pie

1⅓ cups crushed 2¾″ chocolate
   wafers
3 tablesp. melted butter or
   margarine
1 pkg. instant chocolate pudding
1 pkg. instant vanilla pudding
1½ cups milk
1 pt. soft coffee ice cream

1. **Early in day:** In greased 9″ pie plate, mix together chocolate-wafer crumbs and butter till crumbly. With back of spoon, press mixture to bottom and side of pie plate.
2. In large electric-mixer bowl, with mixer at medium speed, or "cream," beat chocolate and vanilla puddings with milk until smooth and thickened—about 2 min. Add ice cream and continue beating until blended.
3. Pour into pie shell. Refrigerate at least 4 hrs. before serving.

Baked-Alaska Pie

(*Pictured on page 52*)

Baked 9″ pie shell, pages 4–7
16 large marshmallows
1 tablesp. water or canned pineapple juice
2 egg whites
¼ cup granulated sugar
¼ teasp. salt
2 cups chilled fresh raspberries or
drained, just thawed frozen raspberries or strawberries
1 qt. firm vanilla, peach or pistachio
ice cream

Refrigerate pie shell until well chilled. Preheat broiler 10 min., or as manufacturer directs. Over low heat, heat marshmallows with water, folding constantly, until marshmallows are melted. Beat egg whites until quite stiff; gradually add sugar and salt, beating until very stiff; fold in marshmallow mixture. Sprinkle 1 cup berries into pie shell; fill with ice cream; then sprinkle rest of berries onto ice cream; top with meringue, covering ice cream completely all the way around out to edge of pie, (this helps keep ice cream firm). Broil several inches below heat until lightly browned. Serve at once.

Note—If you have a freezer, you can make this pie several days ahead. Just make as above, omitting berries. As soon as meringue has browned, place pie in freezer until frozen; then freezer-wrap, and return to freezer. To serve, remove from freezer about 45 min. ahead of serving. Unwrap and let stand at room temperature. Use frozen raspberries, or sweeten fresh ones a bit, and serve as sauce over pie wedges. (For variety, use any favorite ice-cream flavor. Let guests top their pie wedges with choice of sundae sauces.)

Ellen's Sundae Pie

(*Pictured on page 49*)

¾ roll packaged, refrigerated but-
terscotch-nut or coconut icebox
cookie dough
Chocolate Sauce, below
1 qt. vanilla ice cream
3 egg whites
Pinch salt
6 tablesp. granulated sugar

1. *Early in day:* In 9″ pie plate, make and bake cookie pie crust as directed on inside of cookie-dough label. Refrigerate until well chilled.
2. Make Chocolate Sauce; refrigerate.
3. *At serving time:* Start heating oven to 500°F.
4. Fill chilled pie shell with ice cream; refrigerate.
5. In small mixer bowl, with electric mixer at high speed, beat egg whites with salt until soft peaks form when beater is raised. While still beating, gradually add sugar. Continue beating until meringue stands in stiff peaks on beater.
6. Now, pour all but 2 tablesp. Chocolate Sauce onto ice cream. Then cover ice cream evenly with meringue, being sure meringue touches edge of pie shell at all points.
7. Drizzle rest of Chocolate Sauce over meringue, cutting through with knife, to give marbled effect.
8. Bake pie 2 min., or until lightly browned. Serve at once.

For Chocolate Sauce: In double boiler, over hot, *not boiling*, water, melt ¾ cup semisweet-chocolate pieces with 3 tablesp. white corn syrup, 3 tablesp. water. Beat smooth with egg beater.

Note—Baked pie may be frozen at once and stored up to 3 days. Let thaw in refrigerator about 1 hr. before serving.

Raspberry Cream Pie

There's no crust to make!

Line bottom and side of 8″ pie plate with packaged vanilla wafers. Drain *well* 1 pkg. thawed frozen raspberries; to juice, add enough water to make 1½ cups. Use to prepare 1 pkg. Danish dessert as package directs. Into boiling dessert, stir berries and 1 cup sour cream. Pour over wafers. Refrigerate about 4 hrs., or until set. Spread top with whipped cream and flaked coconut.

Macaroon Pie

Start heating oven to 350°F. Finely crush 12 saltines. Finely snip 1 doz. pitted dates. Finely chop ½ cup pecans. Combine all with ¼ teasp. double-acting baking powder, 1 teasp. almond extract, 1 cup granulated sugar. Beat 3 egg whites until stiff; gently fold in date mixture. Turn into well-greased 9″ pie plate. Bake 30 min. Cool. Serve with unsweetened whipped cream.
P.S.—You may double recipe; bake mixture in 2 pie plates; then cool, freezer-wrap, and freeze one or both pies.

Hurry-Up Apple "Pie"

Start heating oven to 375°F. In 8″ pie plate, place 1 No. 303 can applesauce; add 1 tablesp. fresh, canned, or frozen lemon juice; stir. In medium bowl, combine ½ cup brown sugar, packed; ½ teasp. cinnamon; ½ teasp. nutmeg; and 1 cup packaged piecrust mix. Sprinkle mixture on applesauce. Bake 30 min., or until browned. Serve warm, topped with ice cream or light cream.
Makes 4 servings

Kathy's Pecan-Date Wedges

½ cup soft butter or margarine
1 cup granulated sugar
2 egg yolks
2 teasp. milk
½ cup coarsely broken pecans
1 cup snipped pitted dates
1 teasp. vanilla extract
2 egg whites, stiffly beaten
Cinnamon
½ cup heavy cream, whipped

1. Start heating oven to 350°F. Grease 9″ pie plate.
2. In large bowl, mix well butter, sugar, egg yolks and milk. Fold in pecans, dates, vanilla extract and egg whites.
3. Turn into pie plate. Sprinkle with cinnamon. Bake about 35 min. or until silver knife inserted in center comes out clean.
4. Serve, warm or cold, topped with whipped cream. *Makes 8 servings*

Small-Fry Pie

(Pictured on pages 20 and 21)

Packaged vanilla wafers (2″ in diameter)
1 pkg. instant vanilla or coconut-cream pudding
½ to 1 cup heavy cream, whipped
1 or 2 bananas, sliced
Fresh, frozen, or canned lemon juice

About 1 hr. before serving: Line bottom and side of 8″ pie plate with wafers. Prepare instant pudding as package directs. Turn into wafer-lined pie plate. Refrigerate until firm. Spoon whipped cream around edge; into cream, tuck banana slices dipped into lemon juice.
Small-Fry Chocolate Pie: Prepare as above, using instant chocolate pudding.

glazes & toppings

Glazes

Egg White: Brush slightly beaten egg white on top crust just before baking, using crumpled paper, fingers, or small brush. Sprinkle with granulated sugar, too, if you like a glistening, sugary top.

Evaporated Milk: For a good brown crust, brush top crust before baking with evaporated milk straight from the can. Sprinkle with granulated sugar for sparkle.

Cream, Top Milk, Ice Water, or Salad Oil: Brush any one of these on top crust before baking. The heavier the cream, the browner the crust is likely to be. For sparkle, sprinkle lightly, evenly, with granulated sugar.

Butter, Margarine, or Shortening: Dot top crust with bits of one of these; then bake. Or melt; then brush evenly over surface of top crust before baking.

PRETTY PIE TOPS

Star-Spangled (*for chiffon or cream pies*): Bake pastry stars while shell bakes; place on filled pie.

Wagon Wheel: Cut 3 10″x1″ pastry strips. Crisscross to form spokes. Snip out pastry underneath where first strips cross.

Posies (*for one-crust pies*): Cut petals from gumdrops or candied cherries; cut stems from citron.

Sweetheart (*for two-crust pies*): Cut out hearts from packaged cheese slices. Arrange on pie.

Wedge-Apiece: Cut 8″ pastry round into wedges with knife. Prick; bake while shell bakes. Place on the fruit-filled shell.

Cookie Crown (*for chiffon or cream pies*): Make cookie crust; fill; top with a ring of cookies.

Fruit Pin Wheel: Apple wedges on pumpkin; orange sections on cream; peach slices on chiffon.

Swirls (*for chiffon or cream pies*): Swirl whipped cream into "figure nines" gently with a spoon.

3-Egg-White Meringue

(for a 9″ pie)

3 egg whites
¼ teasp. salt
¼ to ½ teasp. vanilla extract
6 tablesp. granulated sugar

1. Set out eggs to warm to room temperature. (Whites beat to greater volume when not too cold.) Start heating oven to 350°F.
2. Place egg whites in medium bowl. Add salt, vanilla. With hand or electric beater, start beating them until frothy throughout. (Don't wait till they begin to be stiff.)
3. Start adding sugar, a little at a time, beating well after each addition. (Added this early, sugar dissolves better, helping to prevent beading.)
4. Continue beating until stiff peaks are formed. To test, slowly withdraw beater and hold up. Meringue should form pointed peaks so stiff they stand upright and don't curl over (*photo A*.

5. With spoon place mounds of meringue around edge of filling. To help prevent shrinking, spread so it touches inner edge of crust *all around*. Heap rest in center (*photo B*); push out to border.
6. With back of spoon, pull up points on meringue to make top attractive (*photo C*). Bake 12 to 15 min., or until delicately browned. Cool on rack, *away from drafts*.

2-Egg-White Meringue (*for 8″ pie*): Use 2 egg whites, scant ¼ teasp. salt, ¼ teasp. vanilla extract, 4 tablesp. granulated sugar.

Meringue Crown: Make 2-Egg-White Meringue. Pile on baking sheet; shape into 6″ round. With help of pancake turner and spatula, transfer onto boiling water in shallow pan. Bake at 425°F. about 12 min., or until delicately browned. Remove to greased rack. Cool.

Unbaked Meringue: Heat ⅓ cup white corn syrup till it comes to a boil. Meanwhile, beat 1 egg white in small bowl till stiff but not dry. Slowly beat in hot syrup; continue to beat till mixture stands in peaks. Add ½ teasp. vanilla extract, ½ teasp. salt. Spread on 9″ pie; sprinkle with coconut, if desired.